The Encyclopedia of

WINDOW FASHIONS

CHARLES T. RANDALL

Randall International
Orange, California

Published in the United States by

Randall International
Orange, California

Distributed in Great Britain by

Antique Collectors Club Ltd
Woodbridge, Suffolk

Fifth Edition

ISBN 1-890379-03-4

How to reach us:
Phone: (714) 771-8488
Toll Free: (800) 882-8907
Internet: http://www.randallonline.com
Email: info@randallonline.com

Illustrated by: Patricia M. Howard
Edited by: Hollie Wheeler and Joy Randall
Layout and Pre-Press Support: Jamey Wheeler
Cover Design by: Elizabeth Randall and Jamey Wheeler
Pre-Press: Kaleido Graphics Inc, Baldwin Park, CA

Printed by: Palace Press Inc

Printed in China

Library of Congress Cataloging-in-Publication Data

Randall, Charles T.
The encyclopedia of window fashions / Charles T. Randall 5th ed.
p. cm.
Includes bibliographical references and Index.
1. Draperies in interior decoration. 2. Window shades. I Title.
ISBN 1-890379-03-4 (pbk.)
NK2115.5.D73 R36 2002
747'.3—dc21
2002002036

10 9 8 7 6

Contents

Historical

1. Historical Window Treatments — 7-15

Italian and French Renaissance 7, English Baroque/Early Georgian 8, American Early Georgian/English Middle Georgian 9, Rococo/Louis XV 10, French Neoclassic/Louis XVI 11, English Neoclassic 12, American Federal/Neoclassic 13, Victorian 14,15

Comptemporary

2. Draperies — 16-49

Over one hundred drapery styles; standard quality features, how to order custom draperies, stack-back chart, yardage chart, window types, pleat-to/fullness charts

3. Valances — 50-71

Over one hundred Valance Styles; rod-pocket, banner, arched, French pleat, tear-drop, Cloud, Balloon, Kingston, box pleated, empire, etc., yardage information

4. Swags and Cascades — 72-93

Over eighty styles: turban, wrapped, open, gathered, knots and tassels; arrangement styles; yardage information

5. Cornice Boxes, Lambrequins — 94-111

One hundred and fourteen styles; measuring information

6. Fabric Shades — 112-121

Fifty Styles; designer creations, Clouds, Balloons, Romans, Stagecoach

7. Curtains — 122-131

Forty five Styles; including various heading and unique valance combinations

8. Accessories — 132-139

Eighteen Tie-bands, six table covers , twenty one pillows/cushions, placemats, seat-cushions, rosettes, lamp shades, napkins, slip covers, wastebaskets, etc

9. Bed Coverings — 140-147

Thirty bedspread/coverlet styles; upholstered headboards, dust ruffles, pillow shams, benches, yardage information

10. Blinds and Shutters — 148-165

Shutters, wood-blinds, mini-blinds, pleated shades, roller shades, toppers, verticals

11. Windows with a Challenge — 166-226

Creative solutions for fourteen difficult to treat windows

Glossary of decorating terms — 174
Glossary of fabric terms — 179
Textile fibers and their properties — 182
Drapery fabrics—look and performance — 183
Conversion chart — 183
Bibliography — 184
Visual index — 185
Index — 224

This book is lovingly
dedicated to my wife
Elizabeth Suzanne Randall
- Queen of Hearts

Introduction

"The eyes are the windows of the soul" is an often quoted poetic expression. The windows in a house, however, can often be an expression of less than perfection—poetic or otherwise. To help you achieve your own perfect window treatment is the goal of the *Encyclopedia of Window Fashions.*

Is one picture worth a thousand words? Graphics have always stimulated the creation and communication of ideas. The uniqueness—and success—of the *Encyclopedia of Window Fashions* lies in combining the presentation of 1000 illustrations with a truly encyclopedic display of window treatments. Fifteen years and one million copies later, this original publication remains the best organized, most effective design aid available. If your profession is interior design, this new, expanded edition belongs in your library, on your work table and with you in the field.

Visual definitions of a particular window treatment are immediately effective communication tools. When accompanied by specific yardage requirements, by glossary-supplied performance summaries of fabric properties and appearance and by alternative approaches to creating a desired effect, you have all the information necessary to work with your client. Whether a budget is lavish or modest, the *Encyclopedia of Window Fashions* offers the optimum number of choices in an individual design situation.

If this is your introduction to *Encyclopedia of Window Fashions*, welcome! Our book is sure to become an indispensable resource tool in your work. If you are among the many who own an earlier edition, I extend my sincere appreciation. Without your patronage, our latest version would not be possible. I know you will find that it continues in the high tradition you have come to expect from us.

Charles Randall

Historical Windows

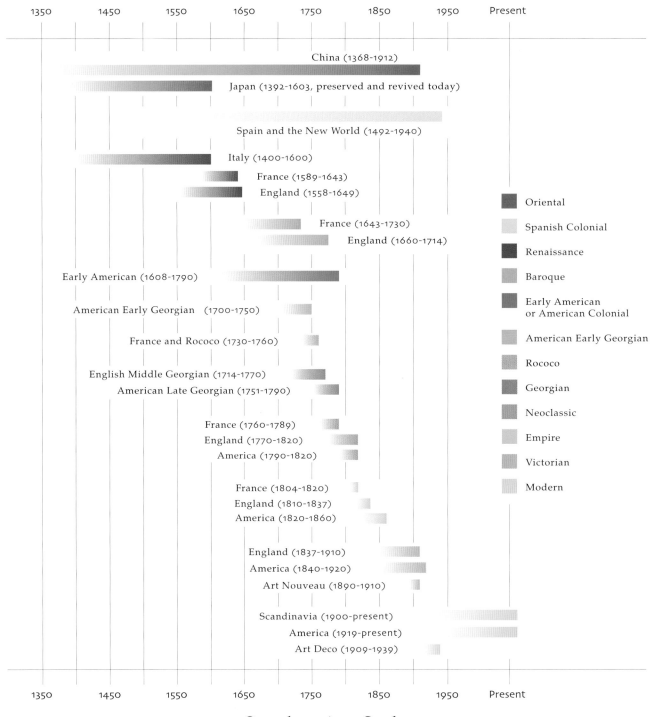

1350   1450   1550   1650   1750   1850   1950   Present

China (1368-1912)

Japan (1392-1603, preserved and revived today)

Spain and the New World (1492-1940)

Italy (1400-1600)

France (1589-1643)

England (1558-1649)

France (1643-1730)

England (1660-1714)

Early American (1608-1790)

American Early Georgian (1700-1750)

France and Rococo (1730-1760)

English Middle Georgian (1714-1770)

American Late Georgian (1751-1790)

France (1760-1789)

England (1770-1820)

America (1790-1820)

France (1804-1820)

England (1810-1837)

America (1820-1860)

England (1837-1910)

America (1840-1920)

Art Nouveau (1890-1910)

Scandinavia (1900-present)

America (1919-present)

Art Deco (1909-1939)

Oriental

Spanish Colonial

Renaissance

Baroque

Early American
or American Colonial

American Early Georgian

Rococo

Georgian

Neoclassic

Empire

Victorian

Modern

1350   1450   1550   1650   1750   1850   1950   Present

Overlapping Styles

Styles overlapped in the market due to new styles appearing at the end of one period while older styles continued to appear at the lower end of the markets. Transitional forms of style may appear in the higher end of the market because newer more technically advanced features are always being added onto the already existing older styles. Styling preferences varied both in different regions and social groups. One example would be the Regency Period, where its style was still fashionable for over half a century in the north, while it had gone out of style over half a century ago during its popularity.

Italian and French Renaissance
1400-1649

English Baroque/Early Georgian
1660-1714

Visual Index p.185

American Early Georgian/English Middle Georgian
1714-1770

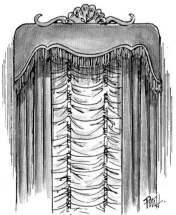

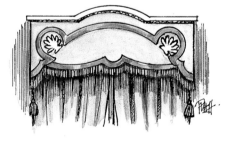

Rococo/Louis XV
1730-1760

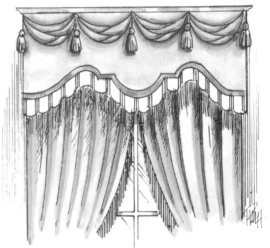

French Neoclassic/Louis XVI
1760-1789

English Neoclassic
1770-1820

Visual Index p.186

American Federal/Neoclassic
1790-1860

13   Visual Index p.186

Victorian
1837-1920

14

Visual Index p.186

Victorian
1837-1920

Visual Index p.187

Draperies

Pointed Valance with Swags over
Pleated Draperies

Goblet Pleated Valance with Tassels
on Dec. Rod

Tab Draperies with Tear Drop Valance
on Dec. Rod

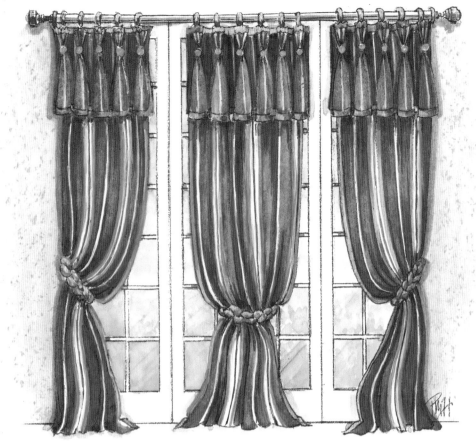

French Pleated Valance with buttons
over Tie-backs

Asymmetrical Valances over Pleated
Draperies and Roman Shade

Tab Valance over Draperies

Visual Index p.187

Various Rod Pocket Draperies

Visual Index p.187

Draperies on Dec. Rod over Cloud Shade

Arched Ruffled Sunburst and Tie-backs
over Café Curtains

Tent Draperies over Café Curtains

19   Visual Index p.188

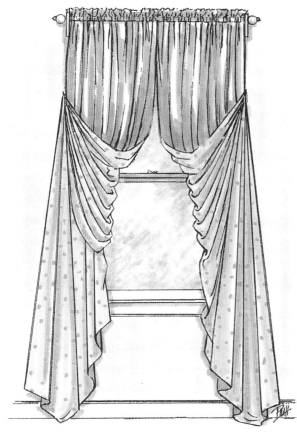

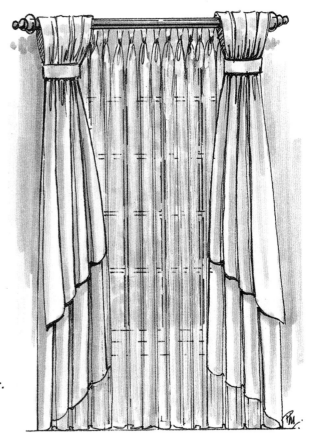

Gathered Draperies Pulled
Back to Show Lining

Tent Pleated Draperies over Café Curtains

Handkerchief Valance over
Asymmetric Tie-back

Draperies Folded and Gathered over Sheers

20   Visual Index p.188

Rod Pocket Draperies under Knotted Scarf Swag

Gathered Draperies over Swag

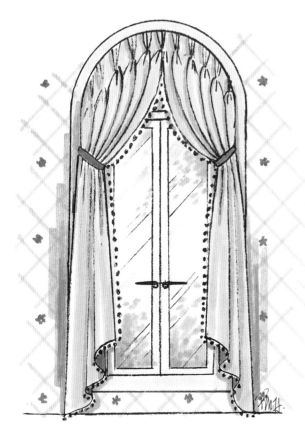

Arched Pleated Draperies

Arched Swags over Arched Pleated Draperies

21

Visual Index p.188

Arched Bishop Sleeve

Arched Rod Pocket Drapery

Arched Knotted Swag Drapery

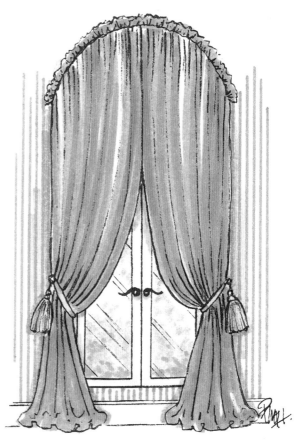

Arched Drapery

Visual Index p.188

Gathered Drapery over Austrian Shade

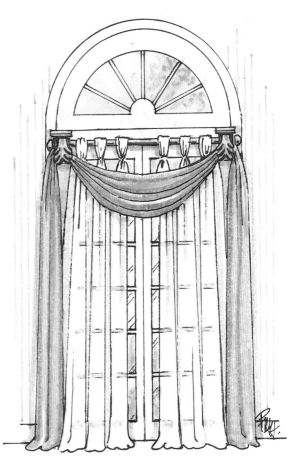

Tab Draperies under Swag

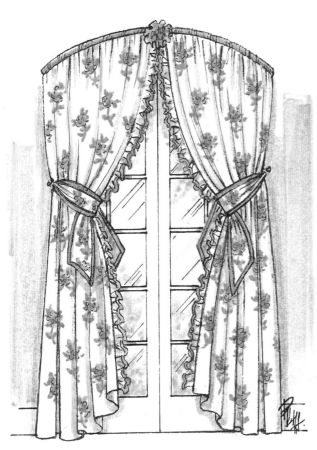

Arched Draperies with Ruffles and Large Ties

Rod Pocket Draperies with Banding

23

Visual Index p.189

Rod Pocket Draperies over Sheers

Rod Pocket Draperies over Cafe Curtain

Rod Pocket Bishop Sleeve Draperies

Arched Rod Pocket Draperies over Cafe Curtain

Visual Index p.189

Pleated Drapery on Dec. Rod with
Tassels and Rope

Rod Pocket Drapery over Sheer
with Tab Valance

Double Rod Pocket Drapery Tied Back

Tab Draperies on Dec. Rod

Visual Index p.189

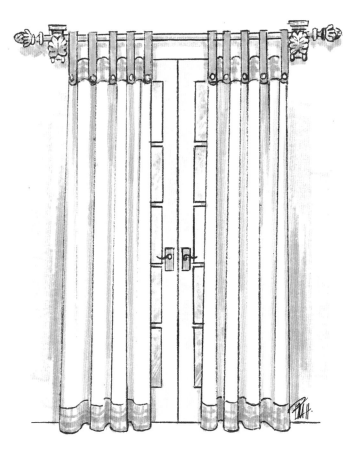

Tab Draperies on Dec. Rod with Sconces

Tab Draperies on Dec. Rod with Holdback

Tab Draperies on Dec. Rod with Holdbacks

Double Tab Draperies on Dec. Rod with Holdbacks

26

Visual Index p.189

Arched Bishop Sleeve Draperies over Balloon Shade

Knotted Lace Swag over Lace Draperies

Arched Gathered Valance over Draperies

Single Swag with Rosettes over Draperies

Visual Index p.190

Tabbed Draperies with Valance on Dec. Rod

Gathered Draperies with Sleeve on Dec. Rod

Draperies on Dec. Rod with
Special Swag Effect

Draperies on Dec. Rod

Visual Index p.190

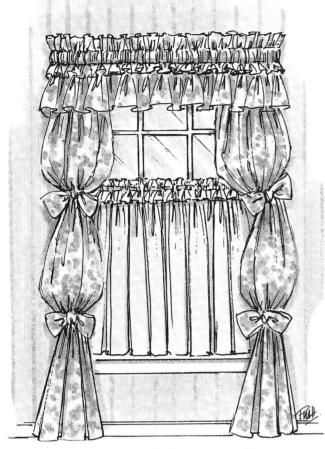

Gathered Valance over Bishop
Sleeve Draperies with Cafe Curtain

Single Swag over Draperies and
Cafe Curtain

Gathered Valance over Tie-backs

Gathered Valance over Draperies

Visual Index p.190

Gathered Valance over Tie-backs

Gathered and Swagged Valance
over Tie-backs

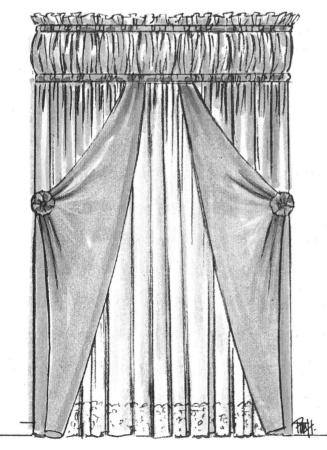

Gathered Valance with Draperies
Pulled Back

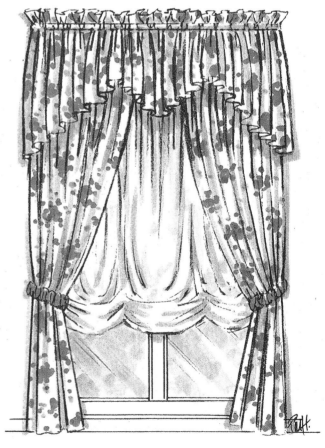

Double Arched Valance over
Tie-backs and Cloud Shade

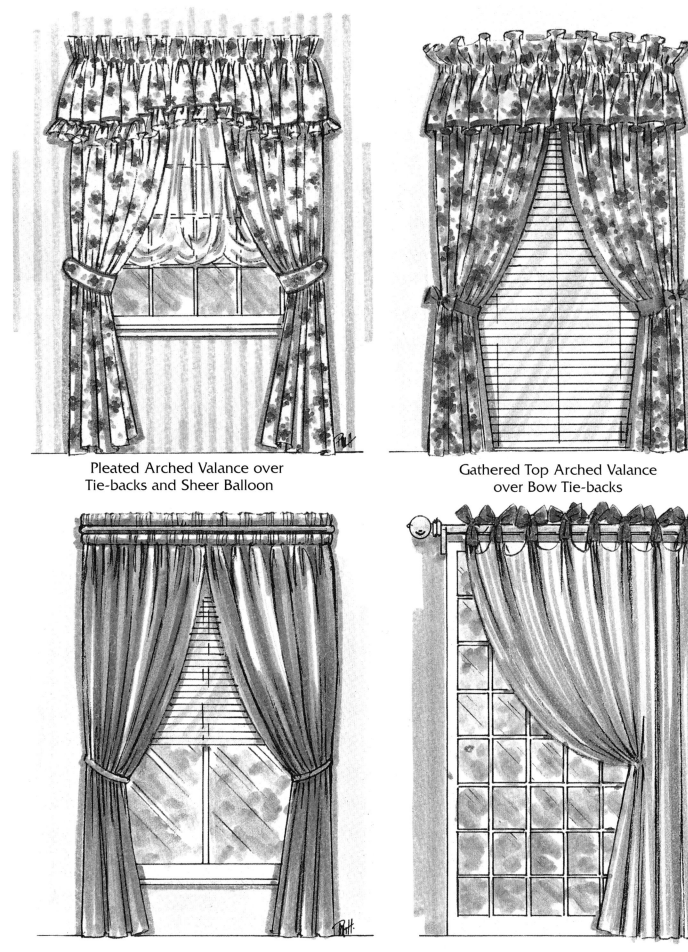

Pleated Arched Valance over
Tie-backs and Sheer Balloon

Gathered Top Arched Valance
over Bow Tie-backs

Double Gathered Valance with
Brass Rod in Middle over Blind

Tabbed Drapery with Bows
and Tie-back Holder

31

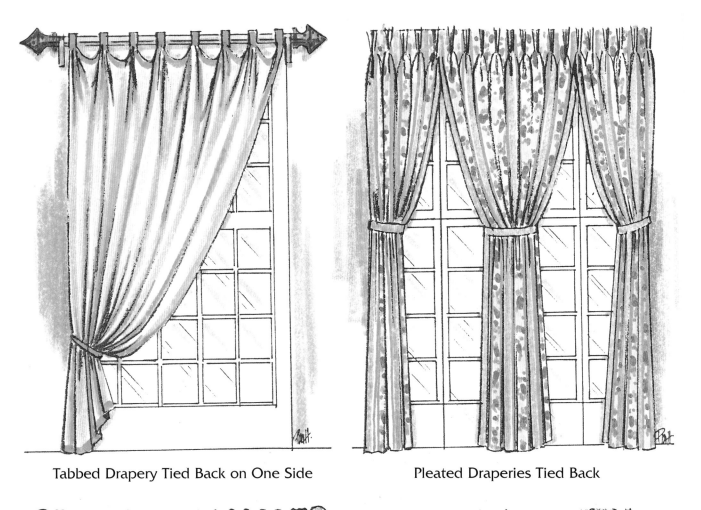

Tabbed Drapery Tied Back on One Side

Pleated Draperies Tied Back

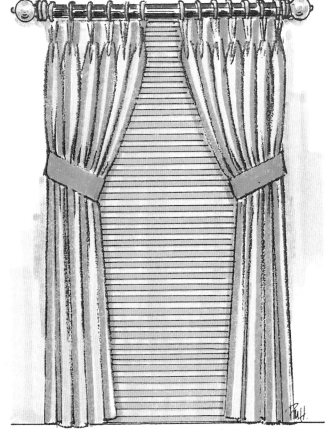

Pleated Tie-back Draperies on Dec. Rod

Rod Pocket Drapery with Tie-backs

Visual Index p.191

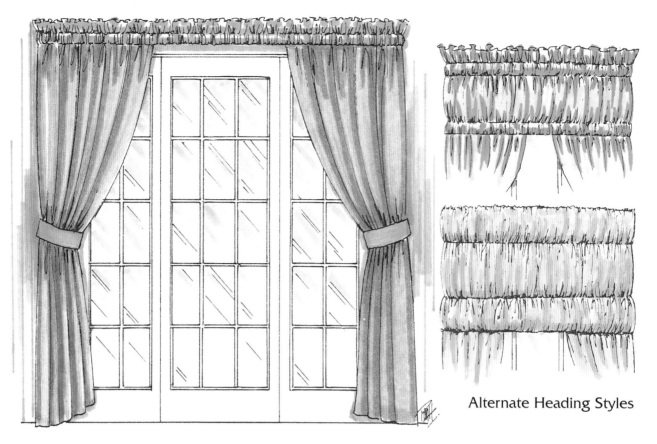

Alternate Heading Styles

Rod Pocket Drapery with Center Sleeve and Tie-backs

Double Rod Pocket Drapery

Bishop Sleeve Draperies with Valance

Visual Index p.191

Arched Valance with Ruffle and
Ruffled Tie-backs over Cafe Curtains

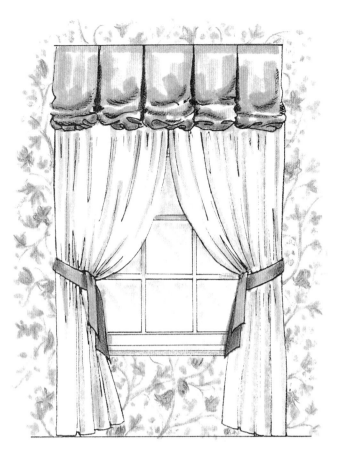

Tie-back Draperies with Balloon Valance

Rod Pocket Drapery with Banding

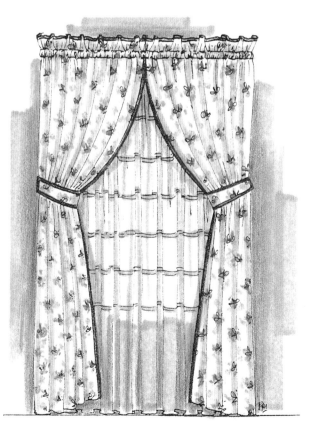

Tie-backs with Ruffle at Top, Sheers under

Visual Index p.191

Flat Rod Pocket Drapery Tied Back

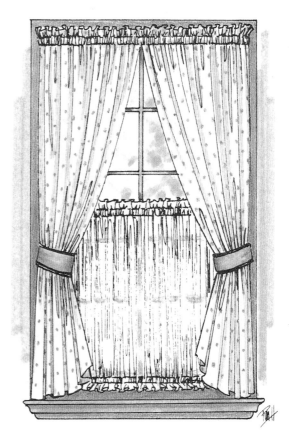

Rod Pocket Drapery over Rod Top and Bottom Cafe

Rod Pocket Tie-backs with Ruffles

Rod Pocket Valance with Rod Pocket Cafe

Visual Index p.192

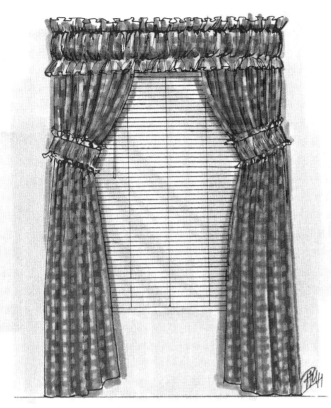

Rod Top and Bottom Valance with Matching
Tie-bands and Mini Blind

Flat Rod Pocket Drapery over
Rod Pocket Cafe

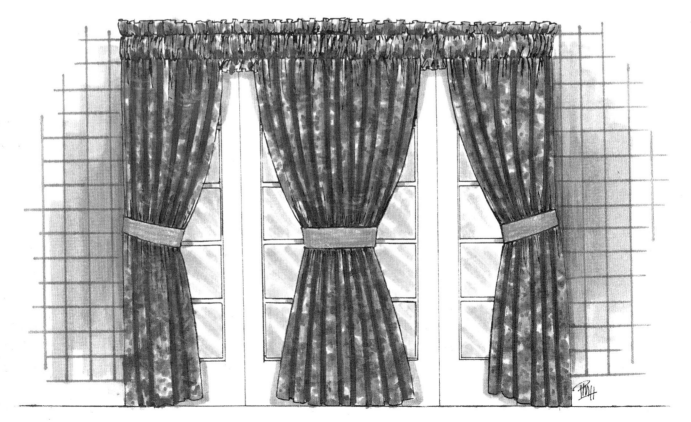

Flat Rod Pocket Panels with Stand-up Top

Visual Index p.192

Kingston Valance over Tied-back
Draperies and Sheers

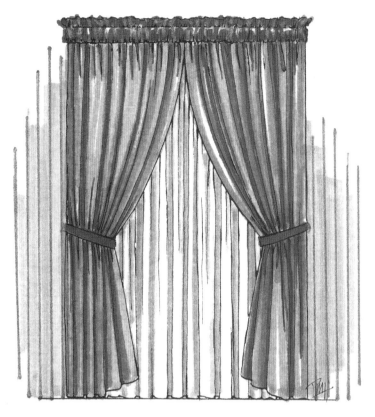

Rod Pocket Drapery over Sheers

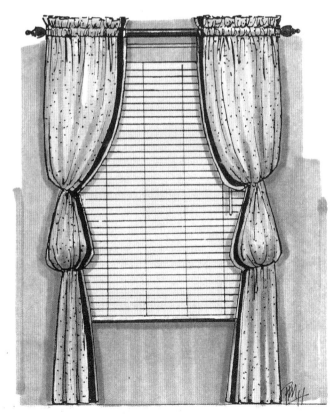

Banded Stationary Bishop's Sleeve
over Mini Blind

Stationary Drapery on Covered Rod
with 3" Stand-up Top

Visual Index p.192

Tied-back Stationary Draperies on Dec. Pole
with Sleeve in Middle

Rod Top Draperies on Dec. Pole

Bow-tied Bishop Sleeve Draperies
Gathered on Dec. Rod

Stationary Rod Top Draperies on Dec. Pole,
Sleeve in Middle

Visual Index p.192

Cluster Pleated Valance on Dec. Rod with
Pleated Draperies over Roman Shade

French Pleated Draperies on Dec. Rod
over Balloon Shade

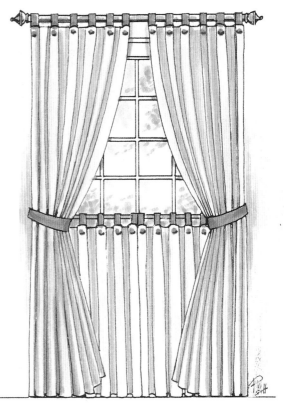

Tab Draperies on Dec. Rod over
Cafe Curtain

Visual Index p.193

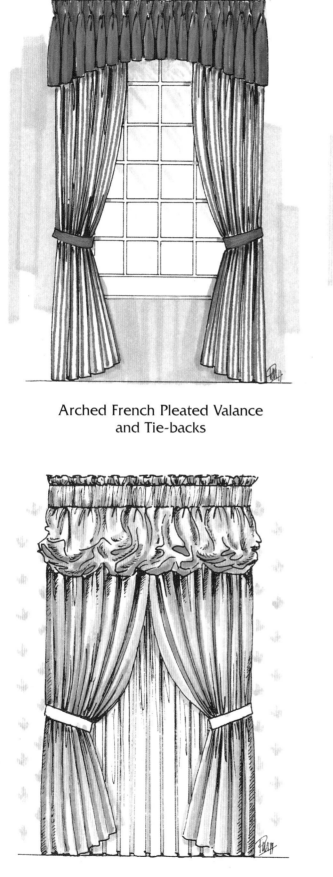

Arched French Pleated Valance
and Tie-backs

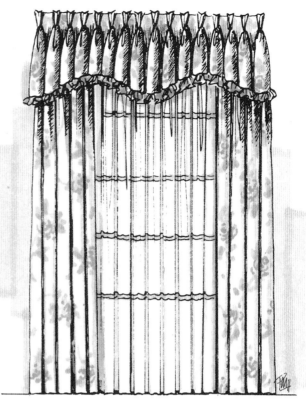

Multiple Arched Valance over
Draperies and Sheers

Rod Pocket Cloud Valance
Tie-back Draperies over Sheers

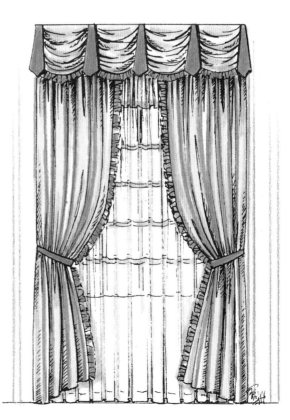

Austrian Valance with Tie-backs
over Sheers

Visual Index p.193

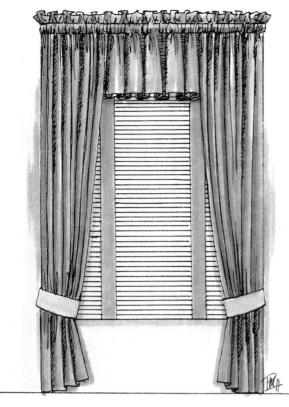

Rod Top Draperies with Center Florence
and Low Tie-backs over Mini Blind

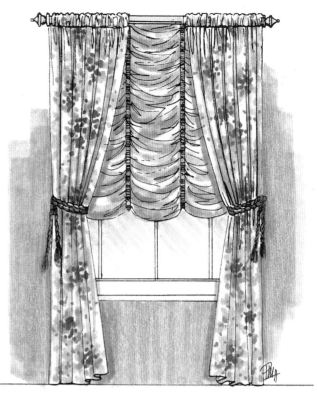

Draperies Gathered on Dec. Pole
over Austrian Shade

Rod Top Draperies with Multiple Bow Ties over Roman Shade

Pleated Tie-back Draperies

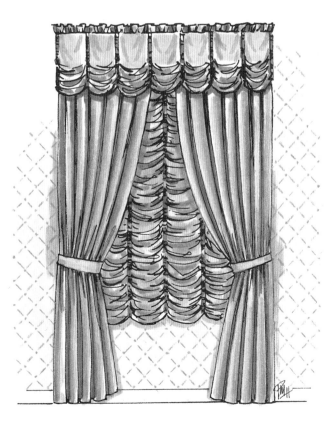

Tie-back Draperies with Austrian
Valance and Shade

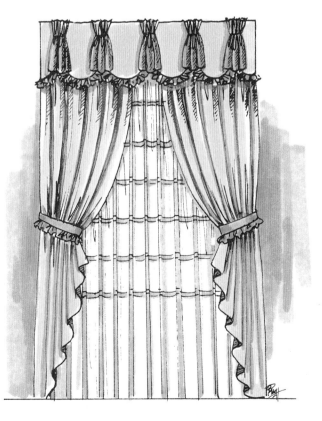

Space Pleated Queen Ann Valance with
Scalloped Edge over Tie-backs and Sheers

Multiple Tie-backs over Cafe Curtains

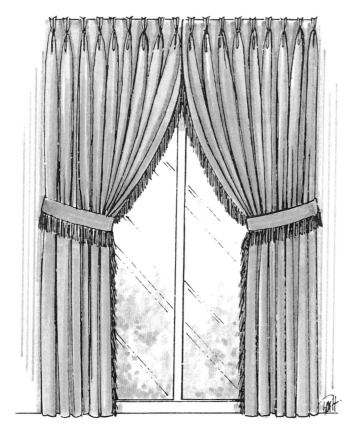

Pinch Pleated Drapery with Fringe

Ruffled Tie-backs with Bow and Rosettes
over Pull-down Shade

43

Visual Index p.194

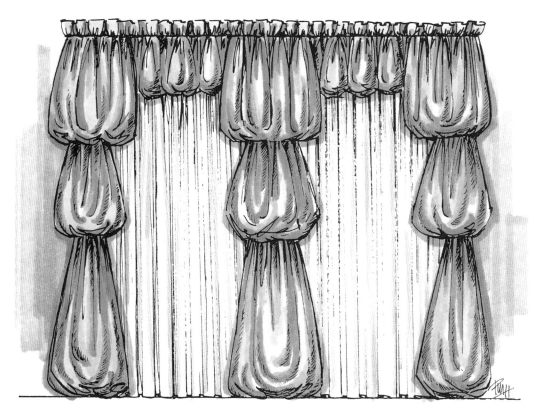

Rod Top Only Balloon Draperies

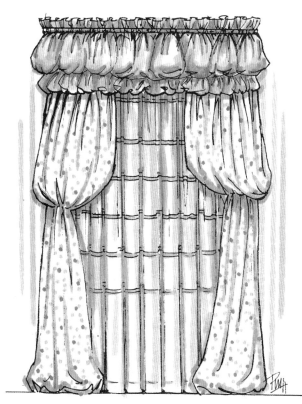

Double Rod Top Valance with
Puffed Tie-backs over Sheers

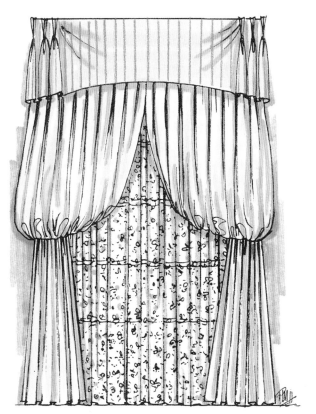

End-pleated Valance with Puffed Tie-backs
over Lace Curtain

44

Visual Index p.194

Custom Made Draperies

Standard Workmanship and Quality Features

- Double Heading
- 4″ Permanent Buckram Headings
- Pleating custom tacked with extra thread
- All seams serged and overlocked
- All draperies perfectly matched
- All draperies table sized
- Blind stitched bottom and side hems
- Double 4″ bottom hems + 1½″ Double side hems
- All draperies weighted at corners and seams.
- Multiple width draperies are pleated so that joining seams are hidden behind pleats.

Made to Custom Measurements

To any exact width or length.
Pleated to any desired fullness up to 3 to 1.
Lined or unlined.

Drapery Terminology

- Width is one strip of material (can be any length) which can be pleated to a finished dimension across the TOP of between 16″ and 24″. Using a 48″ wide material as our base, a width of which finishes to 24″ is considered double fullness or 2 to 1; 16″ finished width is considered triple fullness or 3 to 1. Any number of widths can be joined together to make the draperies properly cover the window area.
- Panel is a single unit of drapery of one or more widths, which is used specifically for one way draw — stack left or stack right — and/or stationary units.
- Pair is two equal panels which are pleated to cover a desired area.
- Return is the measurement from the rod to the wall; in other words the projection.
- Overlap is the measurement, when draperies are fully closed, of having the right panel overlap the left panel. This is usually 3″ for each panel. *Remember your customer must add 12″ to the rod measurement to insure proper returns and overlaps.*

Options Available on Draperies

A variety of Headings:
  Pinch Pleated with 4″ buckram
  Pinch Pleated with 5″ buckram
  Box Pleated
  Box Pleated with Tabs for rod. Add diameter of rod to finished length. For flat tab draperies use 2-1.
  Rod Pocket for shirred draperies.
  Draperies may be self-lined, or
  Draperies may be lined with black-out lining.

Pleat Spacing

Pleat spacings vary according to the widths of material used to achieve a specified finished width. For example: 3 widths of material pleated to 59 inches to the pair will not have the same pleat spacing as 3 widths of material pleated to 72 inches to the pair. If pleats and pleat spacing are to look alike on draperies of different widths, please specify "comparable fullness" on your order. *Vertically striped fabrics will not fabricate to allow an identical stripe to fall between each pleat, panel to panel, or pair to pair.*

How to Order Your Draperies

Since "Made-to-Measure" draperies are made to your exact specifications it is imperative that measurements be made with the greatest of care. We recommend that you double check all measurements for accuracy. All measuring should be done with a steel tape or yardstick. Measure each window separately even when they appear to be the same size. If length varies use dimension of shortest length.

Drapery Width

- Measure width of drapery rod from end to end.
- Add to this figure an extra 12″ to include the allowance for standard traverse rod returns and overlap.
- Standard returns are 3″ in depth. For over-draperies allow for clearance of under-curtain. A 6″ return should be sufficient.
- When ordering panels that stack (draw) in one direction only, specify if the drapery is to stack (draw) left or right.

Drapery Length

- Measure from top of rod, to floor or to carpet. (By inserting pins 1″ from top drapery will automatically clear the floor or carpet.)
- Under-curtain should be at least ½″ shorter than over-drapery.
- When floor length draperies are used it is best to measure length at each side and in the center. Use shortest figure for your measurement.
- Rod should be placed a minimum of 4″ above the window so hooks and pleats will not be observed from outside.
- If sill length, allow 4″ below sill so bottom hem will not be observed from outside.
- When using pole rings, measure length from bottom of rings.

Caution: When both under-curtain and over-drapery are used, be sure to allow for clearance of face drapery. For example, an under-curtain with a 3½″ return requires at least a 6″ return on the over-drapery.

STACK BACK CHART

IF THE GLASS IS	TOTAL STACK-BACK SHOULD BE	ROD LENGTH AND DRAPERY COVERAGE SHOULD BE
38 inches	26 inches	64 inches
44	28	72
50	30	80
56	32	88
62	34	96
68	36	104
75	37	112
81	39	120
87	41	128
94	42	136
100	44	144
106	46	152
112	48	160
119	49	168
125	51	176
131	53	184
137	55	192
144	56	200
150	58	208
156	60	216
162	62	224
169	63	232
175	65	240
181	67	248
187	69	255

NOTE: You will have to ADD RETURNS AND OVERLAPS TO DRAPERY COVERAGE.

THIS CHART IS BASED ON AVERAGE PLEATING AND MEDIUM WEIGHT FABRIC. YOU MAY DEDUCT 7" FROM ROD LENGTH IF YOU ARE USING A ONE WAY ROD. IF BULKY FABRIC IS USED, ADD TO STACK-BACK ACCORDINGLY.

PLEAT-TO / FULLNESS CHARTS

(48" Fabric) 2½ X's Fullness

PLEAT-TO	19	38	57	76	95	114	133	152	171	190	209	228	247	266	285
WIDTHS	1	2	3	4	5	6	7	8	9	10	11	12	13	14	15

(48" Fabric) 3 X's Fullness

PLEAT-TO	15	30	45	60	75	90	105	120	135	150	165	180	195	210	225
WIDTHS	1	2	3	4	5	6	7	8	9	10	11	12	13	14	15

(54" Fabric) 2½ X's Fullness

PLEAT-TO	21	42	63	84	105	126	147	168	189	210	231	254	273	294	315
WIDTHS	1	2	3	4	5	6	7	8	9	10	11	12	13	14	15

(54" Fabric) 3 X's Fullness

PLEAT-TO	17	34	51	68	85	102	119	136	153	170	187	204	221	238	255
WIDTHS	1	2	3	4	5	6	7	8	9	10	11	12	13	14	15

YARDAGE CHART FOR 4" OR 5" HEADING (Cut Plus 20")

TOTAL NUMBER OF WIDTHS PER PAIR OR PANEL

FINISHED LENGTH	2W	3W	4W	5W	6W	7W	8W	9W	10W	11W	12W	13W	14W	15W
36"	3¼	4¾	6¼	7¾	9¼	10¾	12¼	13¾	15¼	16¾	18¼	19¾	21¼	22¾
40"	3½	5	6½	8	9½	11	12½	14	15½	17	18½	20	21½	23
44"	3¾	5½	7¼	9	10¾	12½	14¼	16	17¾	19½	21¼	23	24¾	26½
48"	4	5¾	7½	9¼	11	12¾	14½	16¼	18	19¾	21½	23¼	25	26¾
52"	4	6	8	10	12	14	16	18	20	22	24	26	28	30
56"	4¼	6½	8½	10¾	12¾	15	16¾	19	21¼	23¼	25½	27½	29¾	31¾
60"	4½	6¾	9	11¼	13½	15¾	18	20	22¼	24½	26¾	29	31¼	33½
64"	4¾	7	9½	11¾	14	16½	18¾	21	23½	25¾	28	30½	32¾	35
68"	5	7½	10	12¼	14¾	17¼	19¾	22	24½	27	29½	32	34¼	36¾
72"	5¼	7¾	10¼	13	15½	18	20½	23	25¾	28¼	30¾	33¼	36	38½
76"	5½	8	10¾	13½	16	18¾	21½	24	26¾	29½	32	34¾	37½	40
80"	5¾	8½	11¼	14	16¾	19½	22¼	25	28	30¾	33½	36¼	39	41¾
84"	6	8¾	11¾	14½	17½	20¼	23¼	26	29	32	34¾	37¾	40½	43½
88"	6	9	12	15	18	21	24	27	30	33	36	39	42	45
92"	6¼	9½	12½	15¾	18¾	22	25	28	31¼	34¼	37½	40½	43¾	46¾
96"	6½	9¾	13	16¼	19½	22¾	26	29	32¼	35½	38¾	42	45¼	48½
100"	6¾	10	13½	16¾	20	23½	26¾	30	33½	36¾	40	43½	46¾	50
104"	7	10½	14	17¼	20¾	24¼	27¾	31	34½	38	41½	45	48¼	51¾
108"	7¼	10¾	14¼	18	21½	25	28½	32	35¾	39¼	42¾	46¼	50	53½

RTB . . . . Cut Plus 12"   TIE BACKS . . . . CUT 12"

YARDAGE CHART FOR 5" HEADINGS (DOUBLE) . . . PLAIN FABRICS ONLY. CUT PLUS 20".

Window Types

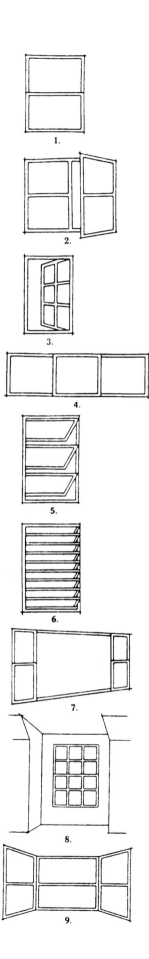

1. **Double Hung Window** — Most common of all window types, has two sashes, one or both of which slide up and down. Unless it is too long and narrow or in the wrong location, this type of window is usually one of the easiest to decorate.

2. **In-Swinging Casement** — Opens into the room. If it is not decorated properly, curtains and draperies may tangle with the window as it is opened and closed.

3. **Out-Swinging Casement** — Opens outward. Both in-swinging and out-swinging casements may be operated by a crank, or simply moved by hand. Out-swinging casements are easily decorated.

4. **Ranch or Strip Windows** — Most often a wide window set high off the floor. Usually has sliding sashes and is common to most ranch type houses. It requires special consideration when decorating to make it attractive.

5. **Awning Window** — Has wide, horizontal sashes that open outward to any angle; can usually be left open when it's raining. Unless it is awkwardly placed or shaped, it's an easy one to decorate.

6. **Jalousie Window** — Identified by narrow, horizontal strips of glass that open by means of a crank to any desired angle. Decorating problems result only when the shape or location is unusual.

7. **Picture Window** — One designed to frame an outside view. It may consist of one large, fixed pane of glass, in which case the window cannot be opened. Or it may have movable sections on one or both sides of a fixed pane — or above and below — which can be opened for ventilation. Sometimes there are decorating problems, but in general, a picture window is your big opportunity.

8. **Dormer Window** — Usually a small window projecting from the house in an alcove-like extension of the room. It requires a treatment all its own.

9. **Bay Windows** — Three or more windows set at an angle to each other in a recessed area. You can use lots of imagination with bay windows.

10. **Bow Window** — A curved window, sometimes called a circular bay.

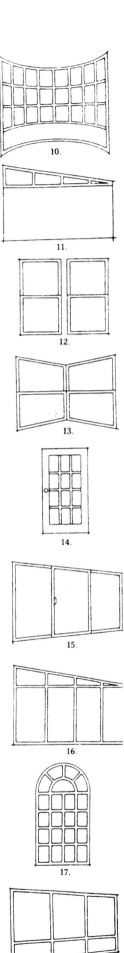

11. **Slanting Window** — Often called "cathedral" window, usually an entire wall of the room. Its main characteristic is the angle at the top where the window follows the line of a slanting roof. This top slanting line often causes decorating concern, but the problem can be solved very effectively.

12. **Double Windows** — Side by side windows. (If there are more than one they are often called multiple windows.) Most often treated as a single unit, always think of them together, as one decorating element.

13. **Corner Windows** — Any window that comes together at the corner of a room.

14. **French Doors** — Sometimes called French windows. They come in pairs and often open onto a porch or patio. Usually they need special decorating to look their best.

15. **Sliding Glass Doors** — Today's functional version of French doors. They are often set into a regular wall, but are sometimes part of a modern "glass wall." Either way, they need special decor that allows them to serve as doors yet provide nighttime privacy.

16. **Clerestory Window** — A shallow window set near the ceiling. Usually should be decorated inconspicuously. (In modern architecture, it is sometimes placed in the slope of a beamed ceiling, in which case it should rarely be decorated at all.)

17. **Palladian Window** — An arched top window with straight panes below the arch.

18 **Glass Wall** — Usually a group of basic window units made to fit together, forming a veritable "wall" of windows. Curtains and draperies often require special planning.

Valances

Box Pleated Valance with Buttons

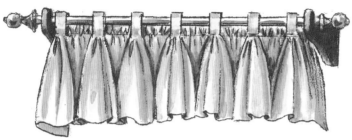

Tab Valance on Dec. Rod

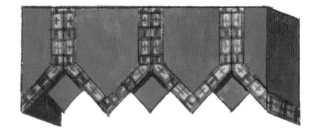

Box Pleated Valance with Points
and Banding

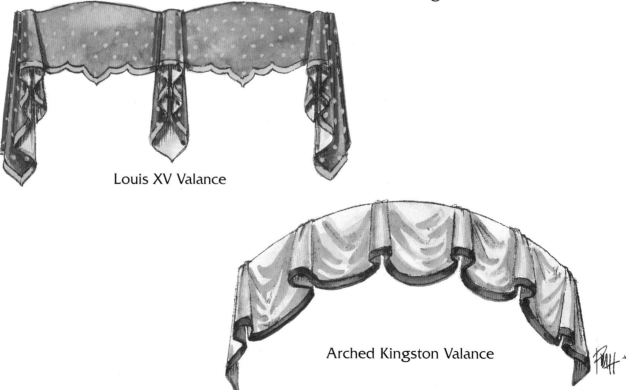

Louis XV Valance

Arched Kingston Valance

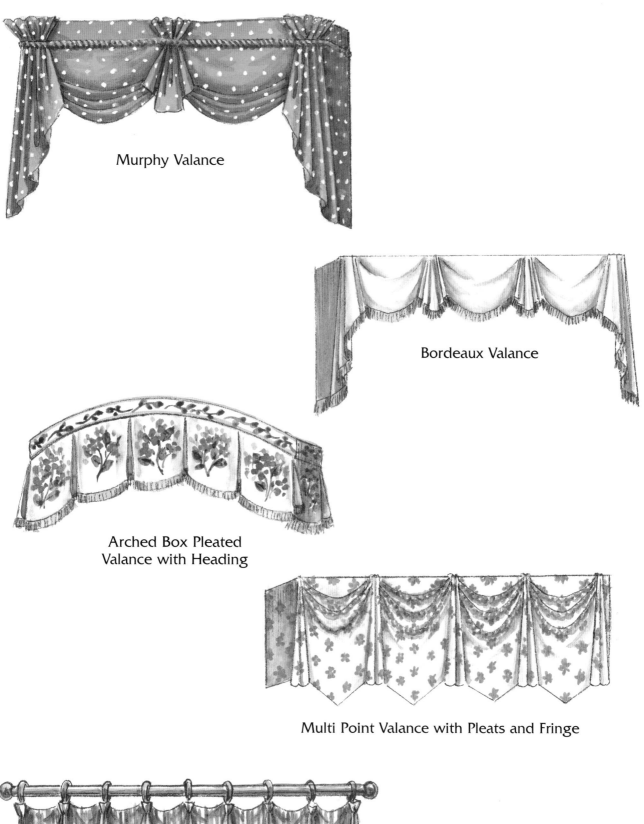

Murphy Valance

Bordeaux Valance

Arched Box Pleated
Valance with Heading

Multi Point Valance with Pleats and Fringe

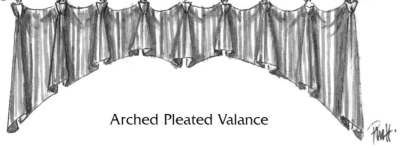

Arched Pleated Valance

Visual Index p.194

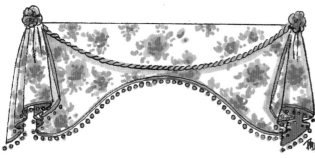

Arched and Gathered Valance with Rope

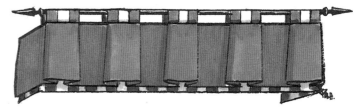

Box Pleated Valance with Tabs

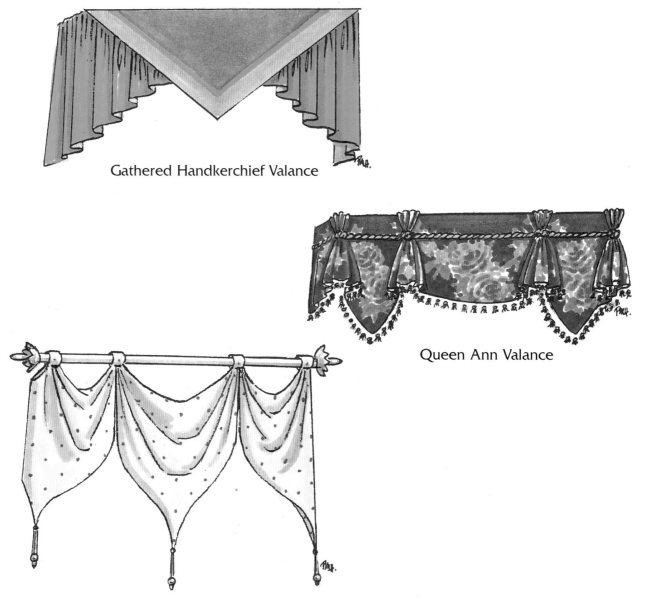

Gathered Handkerchief Valance

Queen Ann Valance

Tear Drop Valance

Visual Index p.195

Open Kingston Valance on Dec. Rod

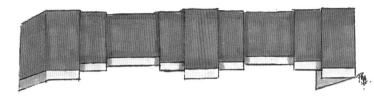

Multi-level Box Pleated Valance

Soft Cornice with Banners

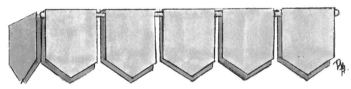

Banner Valance

Scalloped Tabbed Valance with Trim

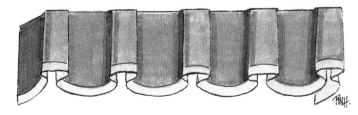

Regal Valance

Rod Pocket Multiple Arched Valance

Rolled Stagecoach Valance
with Wide Knotted Tie Bands

Swags and Jabots over Soft Cornice

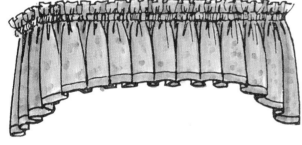

Rod Pocket Arched Valance

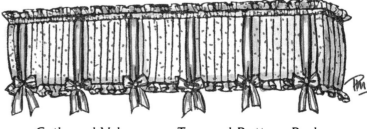

Gathered Valance on Top and Bottom Rods
with Multiple Bow Ties

Visual Index p.195

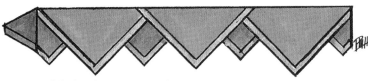

Multiple Point Valance with Edge Banding

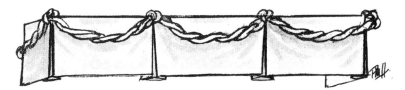

Box Pleated Valance with Twisted Cording

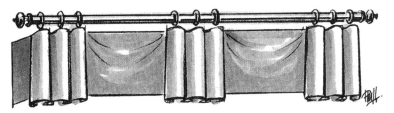

Triple Cone Pleated Valance on Dec. Rod

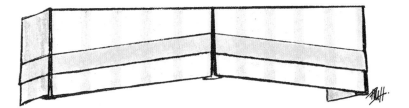

Tapered Box Pleated Valance with Banding

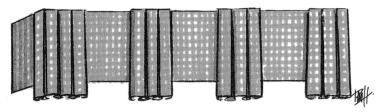

Valance with Triple Box Pleats

Swags and Cascades over Lambrequin Valance

Balloon Shade with Double Knotted Cords

Shaped Valance with Triple Knots

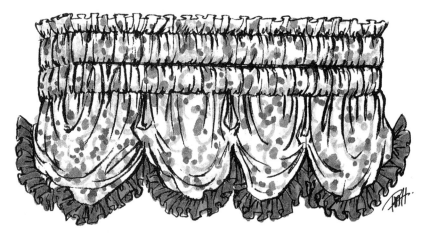

Cloud Valance with Ruffles
on Double Flat Rods

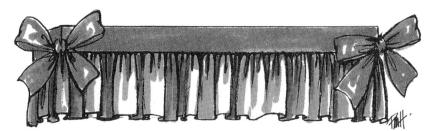

Gathered Valance under Narrow Cornice with
Bows at Corners

Gathered Valance with Dec. Rods Between and
Arched Ruffle Below

Triple 41/2" Gathered Flat Rod Valance

Arched Gathered Valance with Ruffles on
Narrow Double Rods

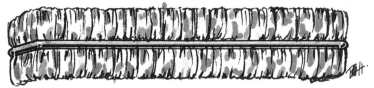

Two Gathered Valances on Flat Rods with Dec.
Rod in Middle

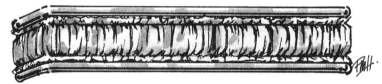

Gathered Valance on Flat Rod with Dec. Rods at
Top and Bottom

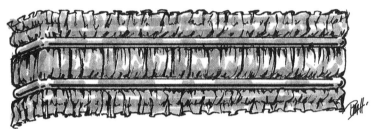

Gathered Valance with Flat Rod in Middle and
Two Dec. Rods Between

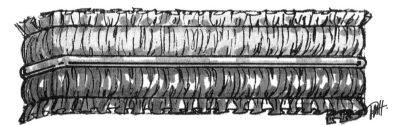

Two 41/2" Flat Rods with Dec. Rod in Middle

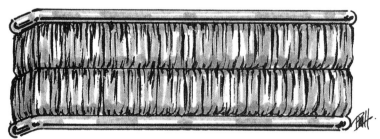

Two 41/2" Flat Rods with Dec. Rods
Top and Bottom

Visual Index p.196

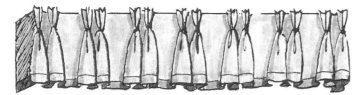

Double Pinch Pleat

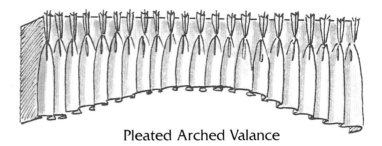

Pleated Arched Valance

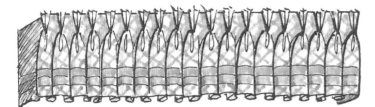

French Pleated Valance

Double Pleat Queen Ann

Spaced Pleated Valance

Queen Ann Valance

 Visual Index p.196

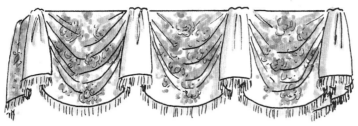

Kingston Valance

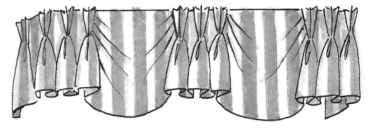

Space Pleated Queen Ann Valance

Rod Pocket Arched Valance

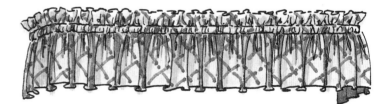

Rod Pocket Valance

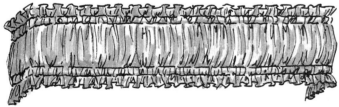

Rod Pocket Top and Bottom Valance

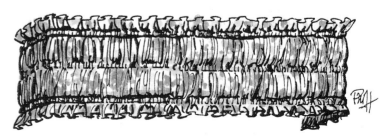

Double Rod Pocket Top and Bottom Valance

Visual Index p.197

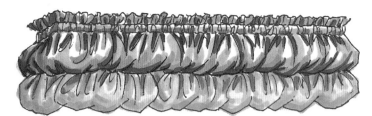

Double Rod Pocket Top and Bottom Valance

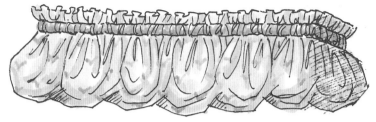

Rod Pocket Top and Bottom Valance
with Lower Rod Lifted

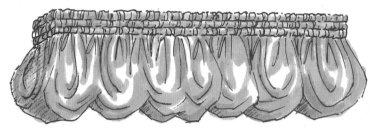

Cloud Valance with Shirred Heading

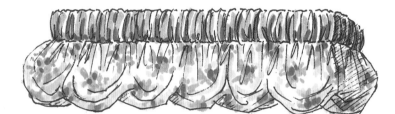

Cloud Valance with Rod Pocket Heading

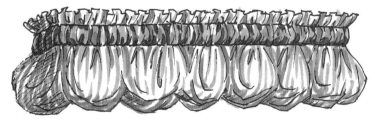

Cloud Valance with Stand-up Ruffle

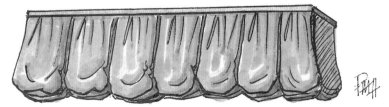

Balloon Valance with Piping

Rod Top Swag and Cascade

Rod Pocket Tapered Valance

Rod Pocket Swag and Jabot Valance

Austrian Valance with Fringe

Austrian Valance with Jabots

Austrian Valance with Cascades

Visual Index p.197

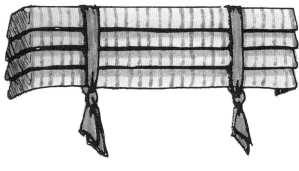

Mock Roman with ties

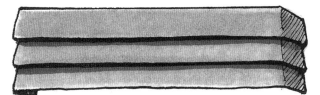

Mock Roman

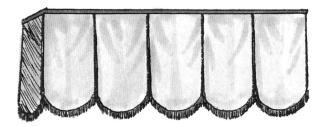

Scalloped Valance with Fringed Edge

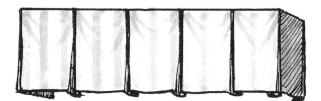

Inverted Box Pleat

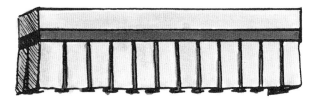

Inverted Box Pleat with Banding

Box Pleat with Banding

Visual Index p.197

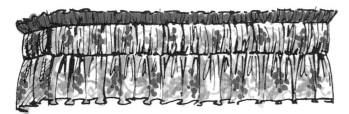

Rod Pocket with Stand-up Ruffle

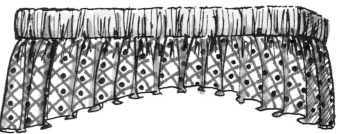

Arched Rod Pocket

Double Rod Pocket with
Stand-up Top and Bottom

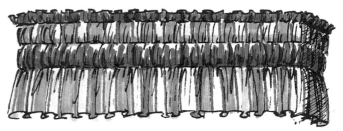

Double Rod Pocket with Stand-up

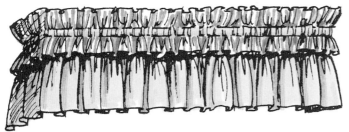

Double Ruffled Valance Shirred on Rod

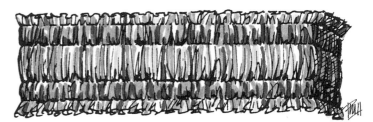

Double Rod Pocket Rod Pocket Top and Bottom
with Stand-up

Rod Pocket Heading with No Stand-up

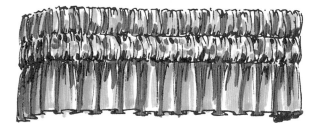

Double Rod Pocket with No Stand-up

Double Rod Pocket Cloud Valance

Triple Rod Pocket with Multiple Fabrics

4" Shirred Heading

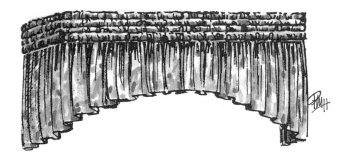

Arched 4" Shirred Heading

Visual Index p.198

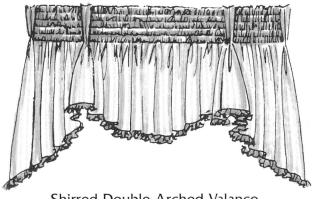

Shirred Double Arched Valance
with Spaced Pleats

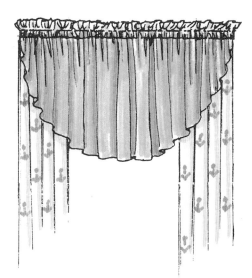

Rod Pocket Spacer Valance

Double Rod Pocket with Ruffles
and Tapered Sides

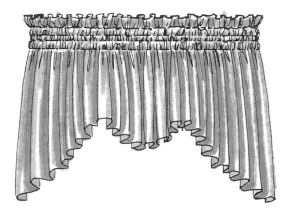

Double Arched Valance with Shirred
Heading and Tapered Sides

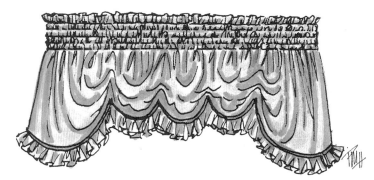

Shirred Cloud Valance with Dropped Sides and Ruffle

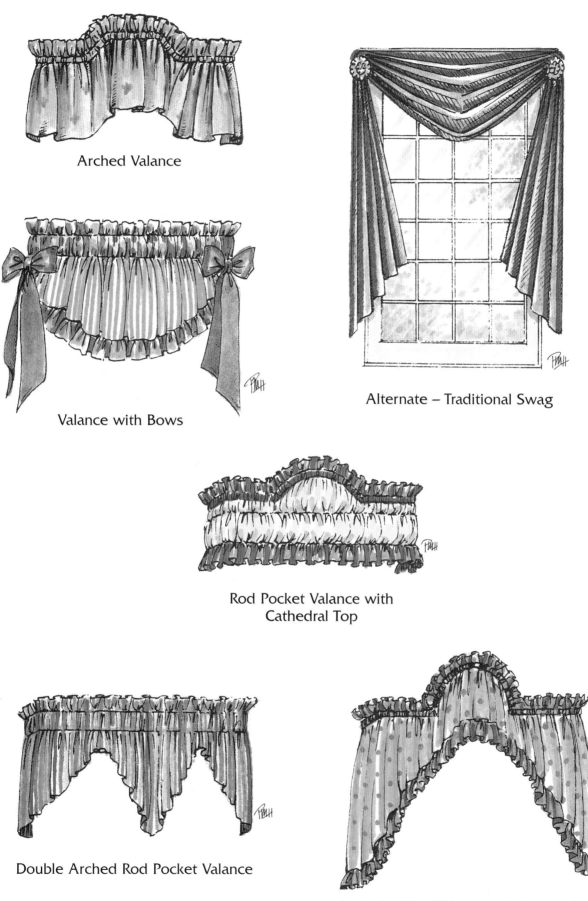

Arched Valance

Valance with Bows

Alternate – Traditional Swag

Rod Pocket Valance with
Cathedral Top

Double Arched Rod Pocket Valance

Cathedral Top Valance with Tapered Sides

67

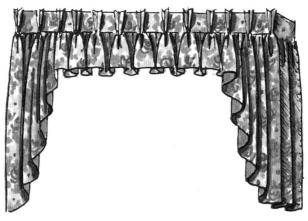

French Pleated Valance with
Tapered Sides

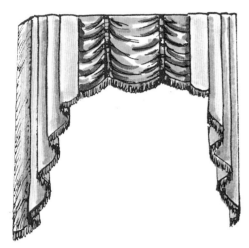

Austrian Valance with
Side Cascades

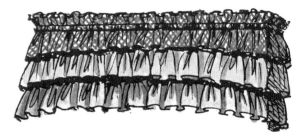

Rod Pocket Petticoat Valance

New Orleans Valance with 6" Ruffle

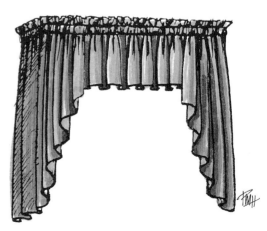

Rod Pocket Valance with Tapered Sides

Visual Index p.199

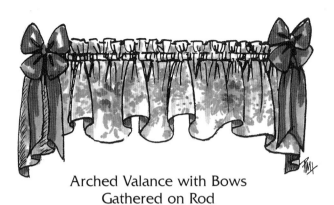

Arched Valance with Bows
Gathered on Rod

Cloud Valance with Stand-up Ruffle

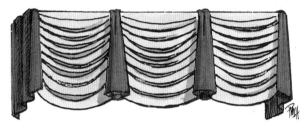

Empire Valance with Jabots

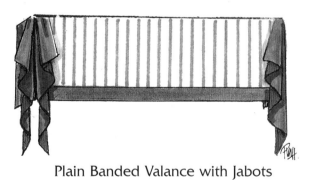

Plain Banded Valance with Jabots

Tab-top Valance on Dec. Rod

Yardage Information

TERMS

Pleat- To: Rod or Board facing plus returns.

Finished Length (Top to Bottom): Length after the valance is fabricated. That is, the length you want the valance to be after the workroom makes it.

Cut Length: Is the length of material figured per width consisting of the finished length plus the number of inches your workroom requires for heading, bottom hem, possible repeat, and allowance for trim off.

Width: Each piece of drapery fabric sewn together to form a pair or panel of draperies is a width. Example, a one way panel of draperies with a pleat-to of 110" requires 6 widths of 48" fabric. See fullness chart below.

Fullness: The more fabric you pleat-to, or gather together to fill a given space determines the fullness. Usually two, two and a half, or three times fullness.

Repeat: How many inches a pattern takes to repeat itself.

PLEAT-TO / FULLNESS CHARTS

(48" Fabric) 2½ X's Fullness

PLEAT-TO	19	38	57	76	95	114	133	152	171	190	209	228	247	266	285
WIDTHS	1	2	3	4	5	6	7	8	9	10	11	12	13	14	15

(48" Fabric) 3 X's Fullness

PLEAT-TO	15	30	45	60	75	90	105	120	135	150	165	180	195	210	225
WIDTHS	1	2	3	4	5	6	7	8	9	10	11	12	13	14	15

(54" Fabric) 2½ X's Fullness

PLEAT-TO	21	42	63	84	105	126	147	168	189	210	231	254	273	294	315
WIDTHS	1	2	3	4	5	6	7	8	9	10	11	12	13	14	15

(54" Fabric) 3 X's Fullness

PLEAT-TO	17	34	51	68	85	102	119	136	153	170	187	204	221	238	255
WIDTHS	1	2	3	4	5	6	7	8	9	10	11	12	13	14	15

General Yardage Requirements

French Pleated, Queen Ann, Space-Pleated etc.
For these valances determine widths required and fullness using fullness charts above. Rod-Pocket/Gathered style valances usually look better with 300 percent fullness.

Self lined Plain Fabric (recommended fullness 2 1/2 - 3 X's)

Double finished length plus 10" equals cut length. Cut length X's widths required divided by 36 equals yardage.

Plain Fabric with Lining

Finished length plus 10", X's required widths divided by 36 equals yardage. Caution: some valances may show lining from certain angles in the room or from outside, therefore, it is best to self-line some valances.

<u>Printed Fabrics with Lining</u> (lining recommended)

Finished length plus 10" divided by repeat, rounded to higher whole number (if number is fractional). Whole number X's repeat equals cut length. Cut length X's widths needed divided by 36 equals yardage. Its better to use lining for print. This is because the print may bleed through in the light if self-lined.

Rod Pocket Valances

Determine widths required using fullness charts. Rod Pocket valances usually look better with 300 percent fullness.

<u>Self Lined Plain Fabric</u>

Double finished length plus 14" equals cut length. Cut length X's widths divided by 36 equals yardage.

<u>Plain Fabric with Lining</u>

Finished length plus 14" equals cut length. Cut length X's widths divided by 36 equals yardage.

<u>Plain Fabric with Lining</u> (lining recommended)

Finished length plus 16" divided by repeat, rounded to higher whole number (if number is fractional). Whole number X's repeat equals cut length. Cut length X's widths required divided by 36 equals yardage.

CLOUD, BALLOON TYPE VALANCES

<u>Plain Fabric with Lining</u> (lining recommended)

Finished length plus 20" equals cut length. Pleat-to X's 3 divided by fabric width, then round to next whole width. This equals number of widths required. Widths required X's cut length divided by 36 equals yardage.

<u>Plain Fabric with Lining</u> (recommended)

Finished length plus 20" divided by repeat, then rounded to higher whole number (if number is fractional). Whole number X's repeat equals cut length. Pleat-to X's 3 divided by fabric width, then rounded to next whole width. This equals number of widths required. Widths required X's cut length divided by 36 equals yardage.

AUSTRIAN VALANCES

<u>Plain/Sheer Fabric Unlined</u>(recommended)

Finished length X's 3 equals cut length. Pleat-to X's two and a half, divided by fabric width, rounded to next whole width equals widths required. Widths required X's cut length divided by 36 equals yardage.

BOX PLEATED VALANCES

<u>Plain Fabric with Lining</u> (recommended)

Finished length plus 10" equals cut length. Pleat-to X's two and one half, divided by fabric width, rounded to next whole width equals widths required. Widths X's cut length divided by 36 equals yardage.

<u>Plain Fabric Self Lined</u>

Finished length X's two plus 10" equals cut length. Pleat-to X's two and one half, divided by fabric width, rounded to next whole width. This equals widths required. Widths X's cut length divided by 36 equals yardage.

<u>Plain Fabric with Lining</u> (lining recommended)

Finished length plus 10" divided by repeat, then rounded to higher whole number (if number is fractional). Whole number X's repeat equals cut length. Pleat-to X's two and a half divided by fabric width, rounded to next whole width. Width X's cut length divided by 36 equals yardage.

PLEASE NOTE

I have attempted to follow the industry standards with the above information. Your workroom may vary in cut lengths, and other requirements. It is best to check with a professional drapery workroom to see if above formulas are acceptable.

Generally, if you want to add lining to above valances then lining amount equals yardage amount.

Swags and Cascades

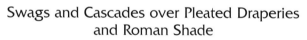

Swags and Cascades over Pleated Draperies
and Roman Shade

Swags and Cascades with Maltese Cross

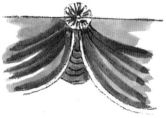

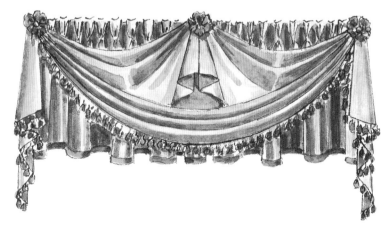

Swag and Cascade over Pleated Valance

Visual Index p.199

Elaborate Swags and
Cascades with Gilded
Heading and Shell Crown

Gathered Fan Swag over
Pleated Draperies

Swags and Cascades under
gold Dec. Rod

Lifted Swags and Cascades with
Cameo Crown and Tassels

Swags and Cascades with Rosettes

73

Visual Index p.199

Swags and Cascades over
Rod Pocket Valances

Swags and Cascades over
Designer Cornice

Various Swags and Cascade Combinations

74

Visual Index p.200

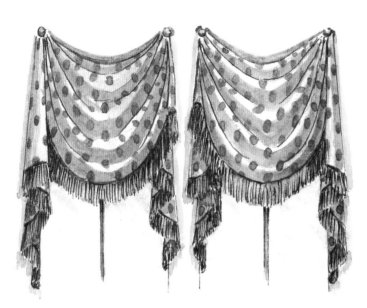

Empire Swags and Cascades

Custom Swag and Jabot Effect

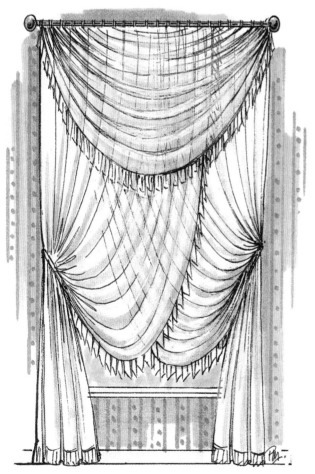

Deep Swag and Full Tie-backs

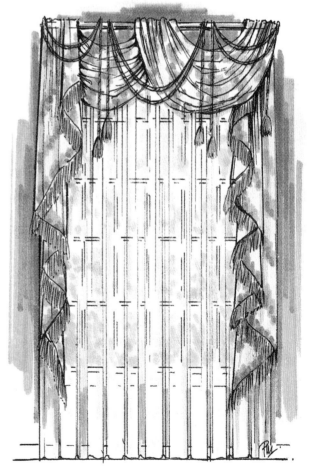

Fabric Swagged over Pole
with Cord and Tassle Trim

Visual Index p.200

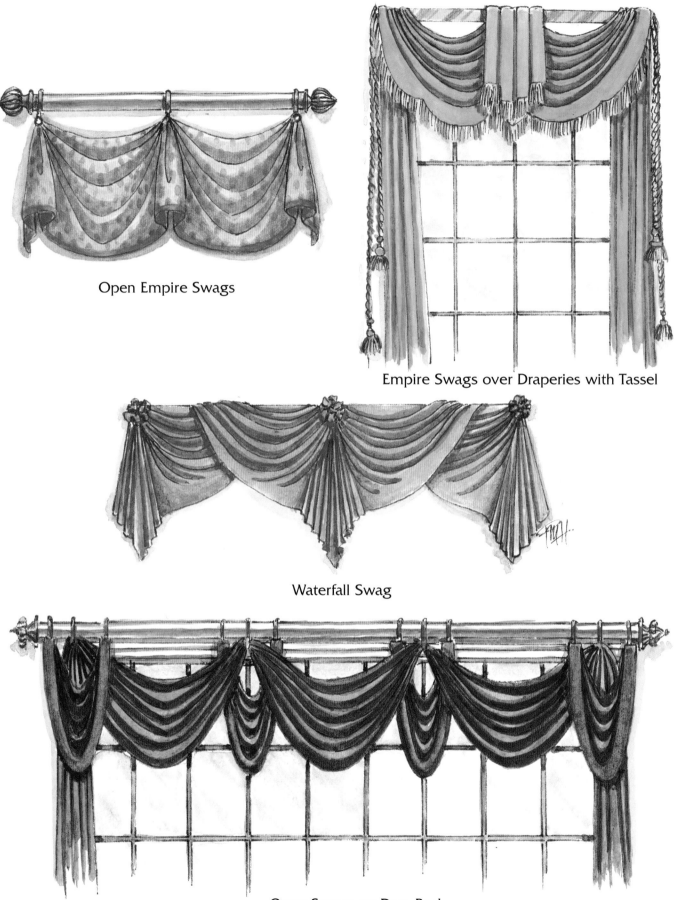

Open Empire Swags

Empire Swags over Draperies with Tassel

Waterfall Swag

Open Swags on Dec. Rod

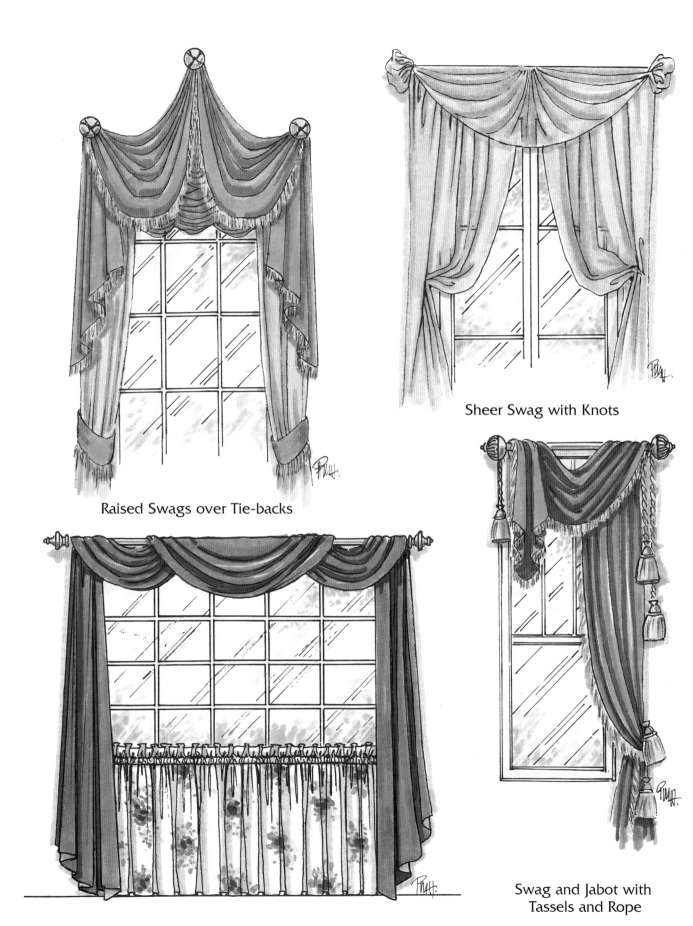

Raised Swags over Tie-backs

Sheer Swag with Knots

Swags over Dec. Rod with Inverted Cascades

Swag and Jabot with
Tassels and Rope

77

Visual Index p.200

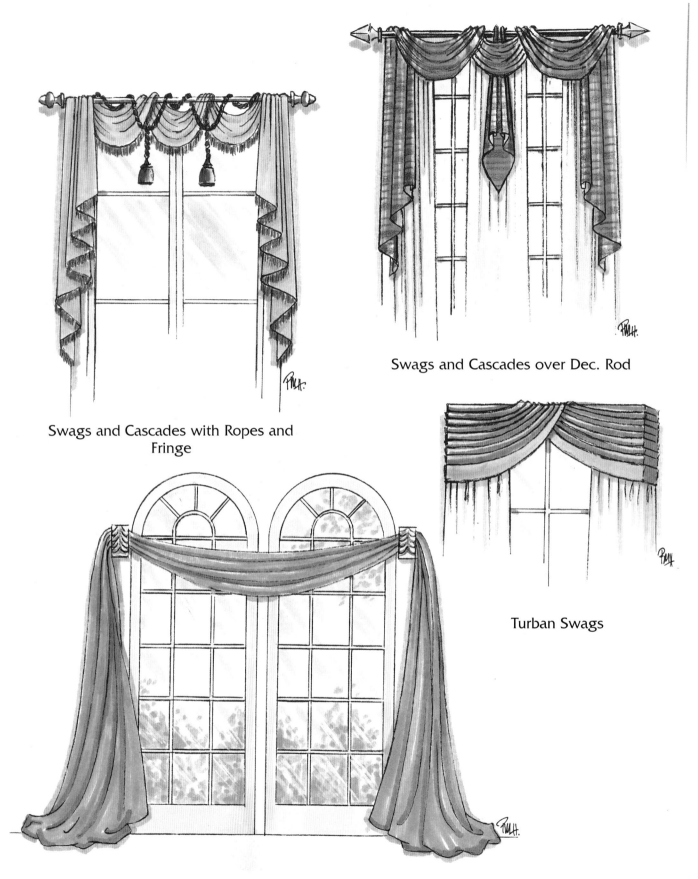

Swags and Cascades over Dec. Rod

Swags and Cascades with Ropes and
Fringe

Turban Swags

Fabric Draped through Sconces

78

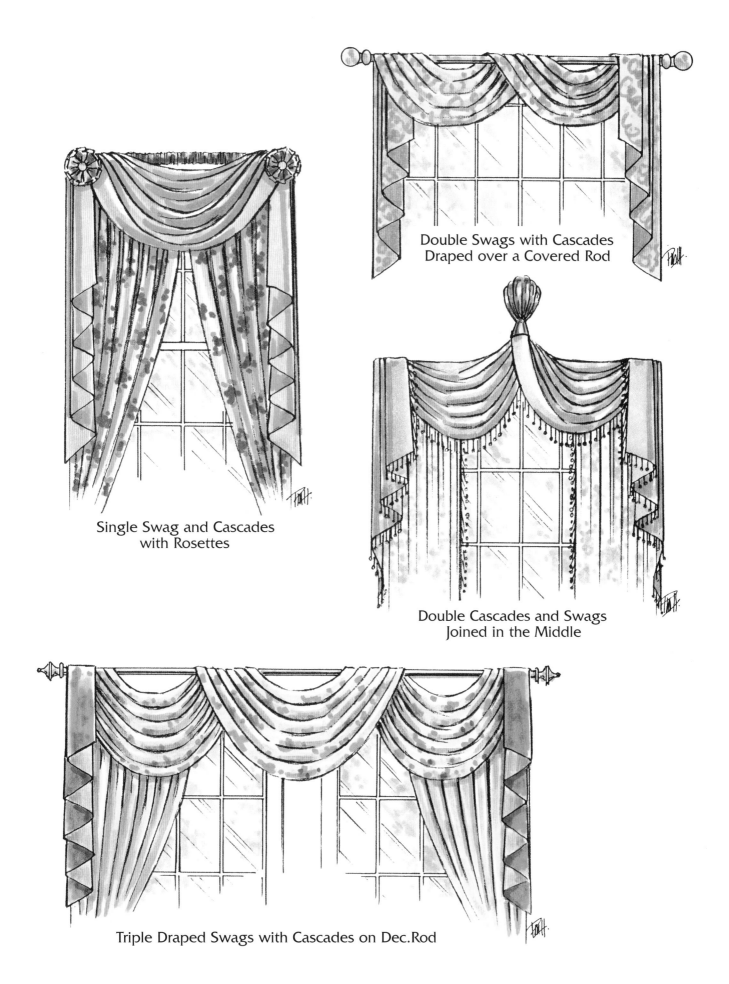

Double Swags with Cascades
Draped over a Covered Rod

Single Swag and Cascades
with Rosettes

Double Cascades and Swags
Joined in the Middle

Triple Draped Swags with Cascades on Dec.Rod

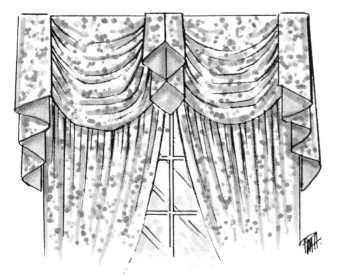

Double Swag with Cascades

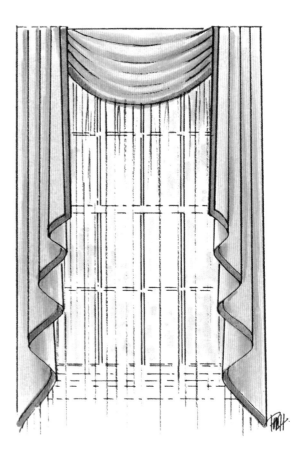

Single Swag with Cascades

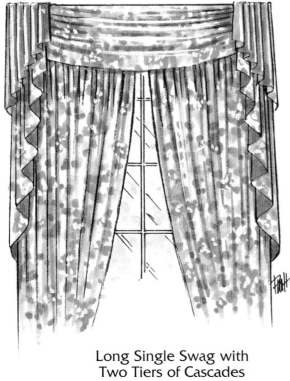

Long Single Swag with
Two Tiers of Cascades

Angled Double Swags
and Cascades with Rosettes

Double Swags Crossed in Middle
with 4 Single Cascades on Rings

Double Swags with Ruffles
and Bows over Cascades

Asymmetric Swags and Cascades

Swags and Cascades with Knots and Tassles

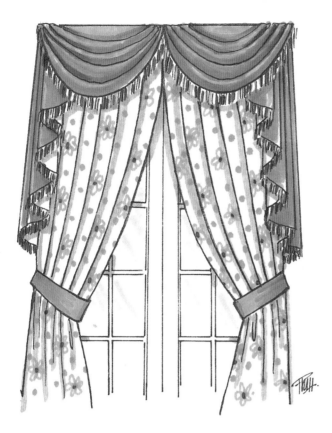

Formal Swags and Cascades

Swags and Rosettes and Center Jabot

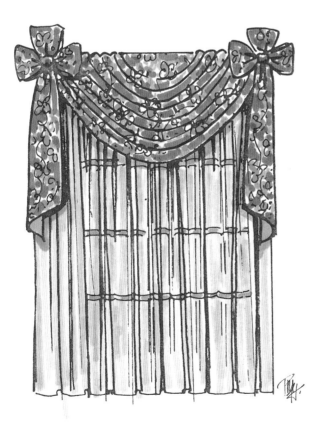

Swag with Maltese Cross Ties

Gathered Swag

Visual Index p.202

Swag and Cascades with Ruffle
over Balloon Shade

Draped Swag

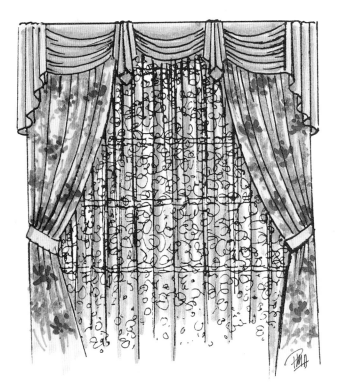

Swags and Jabots over Lace Panels

Swag Draped over Rod

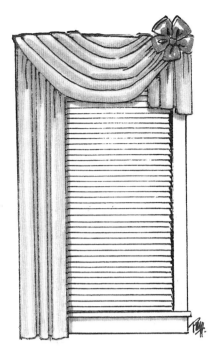

Swag with Rosette and
Asymmetric Cascades

Double Swag with Plain Cascades over Print

Swags and Long Cascades over French Doors

Visual Index p.202

Swag and Cascades with Ties

Swag with Rosettes and Cascades

Ruffled Swag over Tie-backs

Double Swag with Rosettes and Cascades

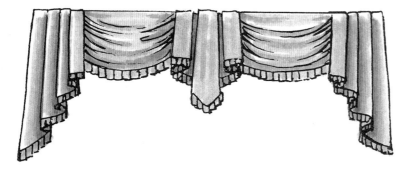

Double Swag with Cascades and Pleated Edge

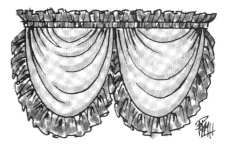

Ruffled Balloon Swag

Visual Index p.202

Swag and Cascade Arrangement Styles

Visual Index p.203

 Visual Index p.203

Swag with Asymmetric Cascades

Boxed Swag Valance

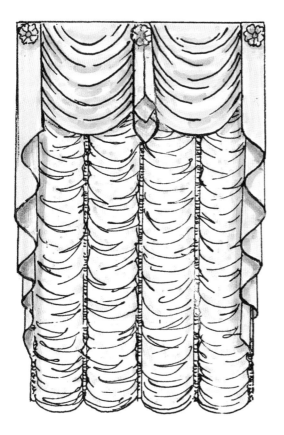

Swags over Austrian Shade

Swag with Rosettes and Bow in Middle

Visual Index p.203

Draped Swag with Contrasting Lining

Swag with Lifted Center
and Cascading Tails

Double Swagged Valance

Single Swag with Rosettes

89

Visual Index p.203

Asymmetric Swag held
by Fabric Ties

Fabric Swagged Through
Large Brass Rings

Swagged Fabric with Cord Trim
over Asymmetric Tie-back

Draperies over Bay Window with
Large Swags Held by Bows

Visual Index p.204

Swag and Cascade Types

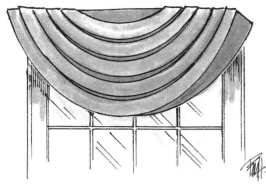

Wrapped Swag

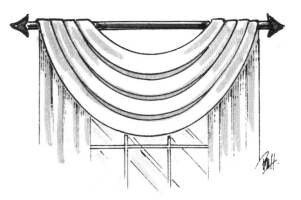

Open Swag

Gathered Swag

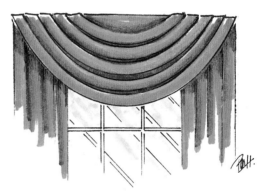

Pleated Swag

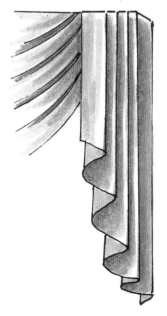

Standard Cascade

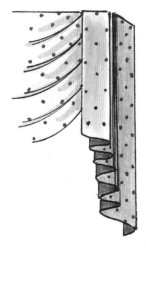

Stacked Cascade

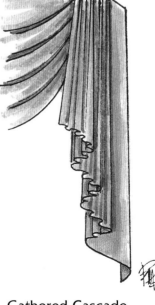

Gathered Cascade

Cascades and Jabots

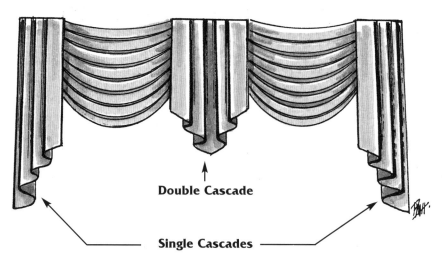

Double Cascade

Single Cascades

CASCADES

SINGLE TRADITIONAL CASCADE

(Yardage is for one cascade only)

Lined in contrasting fabric:
Length: *CL of face=FL (long point) plus 4" extra
          CL of lining=FL (long point) plus 4" extra
Width: Allow one width for face and one width for lining

Self lined:
Length: FL (long point) X 2 plus 4" = CL of face and lining
Width: One width will accomodate face and lining

DOUBLE CASCADE

Length: Contrast or self lined - FL plus 4" = CL
Width: (face) -- one width per Double Cascade(up to 14")
          (lining) -- one width per Double Cascade

Note: *CL = cut length FL = Finished Length

Note: *CL = cut length FL = Finished Length

Jabots are decorative pieces of fabric that are hung over seams
or between swags on a valance. Jabots may be tie
shaped, cone shaped, or rounded on the bottom.

Yardage: Allow approximately one third yard or fabric for each jabot.

EMPIRE SWAG WITH JABOTS

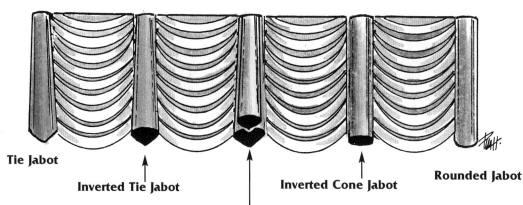

Tie Jabot

Inverted Tie Jabot

Inverted Cone Jabot

Rounded Jabot

Double Inverted Tie Jabot

Swags and Cascades
Yardage Requirements

— Swags

← Cascade

Swags are top treatments or balances, used over draperies or blinds or sometimes alone. They are usually draped into soft, graceful folds, using fabrics that drape easily. It is more interesting to use an uneven number of swags. Swags should be lined.

Cascades are folded pieces of fabric that fall from the top of the drapery heading or valance to create a zig-zag effect. Cascades must be lined with the cover fabric or one that contrasts.

Yardage:
Swags - Based on an average of 44" per swag, you will need 2 yards of fabric per swag.

Cascades - Double the longest length, add 4" and divide by 36. This will give you the number of yards needed for a single pair of cascades.

SWAG WIDTH, BOARD FACE & NUMBER OF SWAGS

Swage may vary in width from 20" to over 70". Very small swags wtih have only a few folds. Extremely wide swags will have a limited drop length. The width of the swag is determined by the board face and the number of swags that will be used on each treatment. The following guide will help determine the number of swags needed based on the board face. The guide to based on the assumption that swag overlap will start approximately 1/2 or less the width of the swag face.

IF BOARD FACE IS:	NUMBER OF SWAGS HELP TO DETERMINE IS:
36" to 48"	1 swag
49" to 70"	2 swags
71" to 100"	3 swags
101" to 125"	4 swags
126" to 150"	5 swags
151" to 175"	6 swags
176" to 200"	7 swags
201" to 225"	8 swags
226" to 250"	9 swags
251" to 275"	10 swags
276" to 300"	11 swags

SWAG WIDTH:
To find the width of each swag, divide the board face width by one or more than the number of swags used and multiply by 2.

Example:
Boards face width = 127"   Number of swags = 5
127" - 6 = 21.16 x 2 = 42.33 or 43" width for each swag.

The standard drop lengths of swags are 16", 18", or 20". Usually 6 or 7 folds are placed across the top of a traditional swag with a standard drop. Swags that have shallow drops of 12" wil lhave 3 or 4 folds.

The chart below is an average guide to help you in finding swag drop based on face width.

IF SWAG FACE WIDTH IS:	AVERAGE DROP WILL BE:
20"	10" to 13"
25"	12" to 17"
30"	14" to 19"
35"	14" to 20"
40"	14" to 21"
45"	16" to 23"
50"	16" to 23"
OVER 60"	16" to 24"

Cornice Boxes, Lambrequins

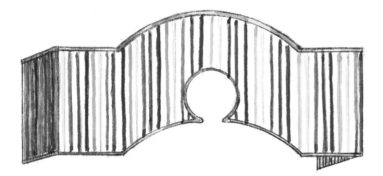

Arched Cornice with Circular Center

Cornice with Banding Top and Appliqué

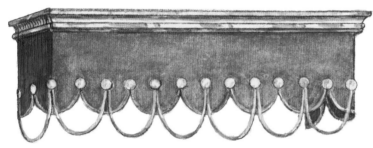

Cornice Box with Gilded Top and Rope Tassels

Designer Gilded Wood Top Cornice

Cornice Box with Large Rope Top And Appliqué

Visual Index p.204

Cornice Box with Appliqué

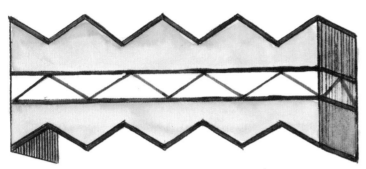

Chevron Top and Bottom Cornice

Pagoda Cornice

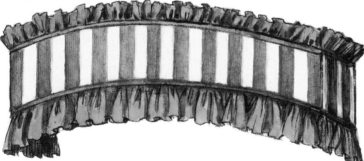

Arched Cornice with Ruffles

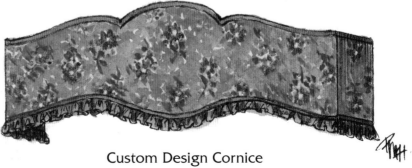

Custom Design Cornice

Button Swagged Cornice

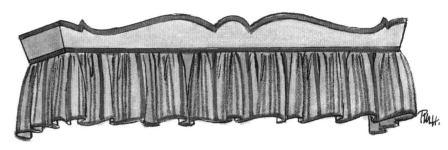

Shaped Crown Cornice with Gathered Valance

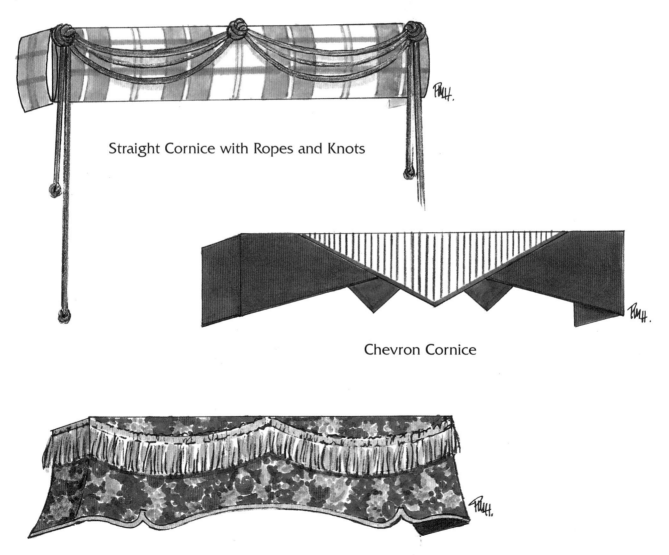

Straight Cornice with Ropes and Knots

Chevron Cornice

Pagoda Cornice with Long Fringe

Visual Index p.205

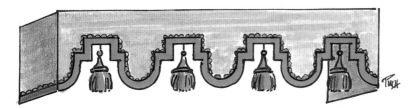

Shaped Cornice with Large Tassels

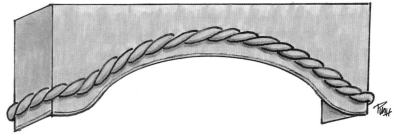

Arched Cornice with Twisted Rope

Shaped Cornice with Fringe

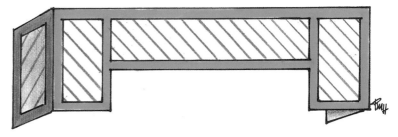

Box Shaped Cornice with Long Side Drops

Multi-Fabric Cornice

Sunburst Cornice

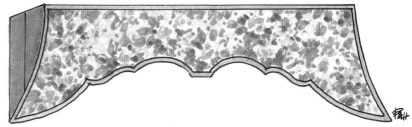

Pagoda Cornice

Straight Cornice with Shaped Crown

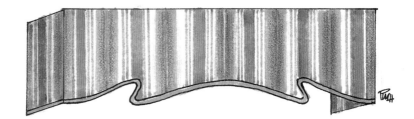

Custom Shaped Cornice

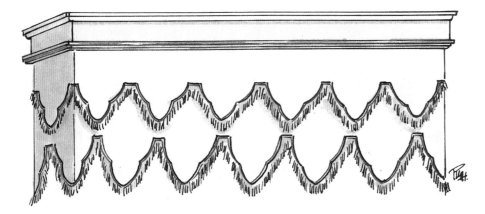

Double Fringe Cornice with Wood Crown

Visual Index p.205

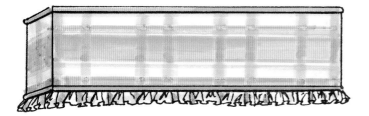

Cornice Box with Ruffle on Bottom

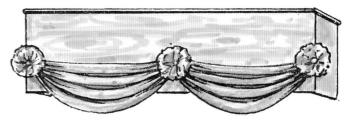

Cornice Box with Swag and Rosettes

Cornice Box with Shirred and Flat Panels

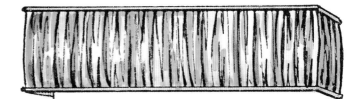

Shirred Cornice Box

Cornice Box with Gathered Fabric in Middle

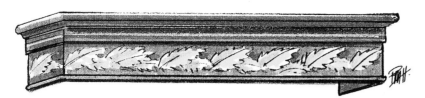

Real Wood Cornice with Painted Leaf Design

Cornice with Real Wood Header

Straight Cornice with Stenciled Design

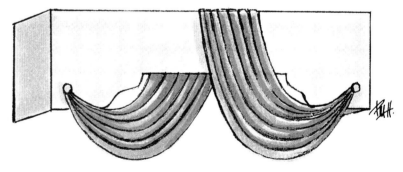

Cornice with In-and-out Swag

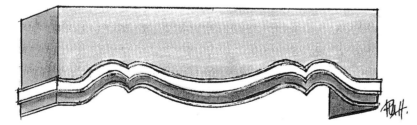

Cornice with Shaped and Raised Banding

Visual Index p.206

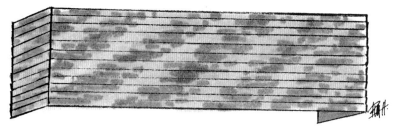

Cornice with Honeycomb Pleating

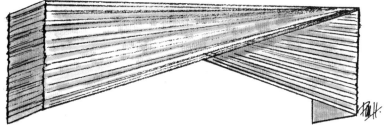

Cornice with Diagonally Arched Pleating

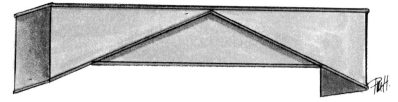

Cornice with Unique Angled Top and Welting

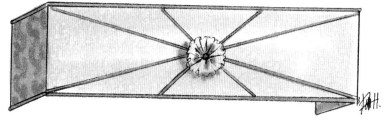

Straight Cornice with Diagonal Welts
and Center Rosette

Cornice with Rounded Gathered Top
and Large Scalloped Bottom

Visual Index p.206

Straight Cornice with Rosettes and Jabots

Pleated Arched Cornice with Special Center Piece

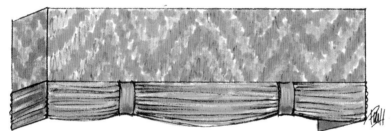

Cornice with Unique Pleated Bottom

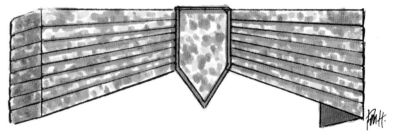

Straight Cornice wtih Gathered Hourglass and Rosette

Cornice with Center Jabot

Visual Index p.206

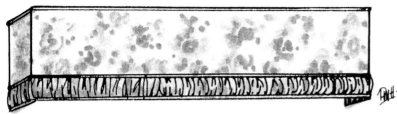

Cornice Box with Shirred Bottom Band

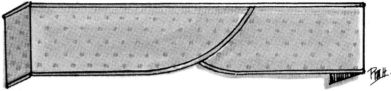

Cornice Box with Special Welting

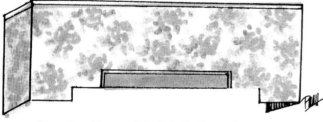

Scalloped Bottom with Banding

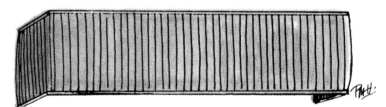

Cornice Box with 1"Pleaes

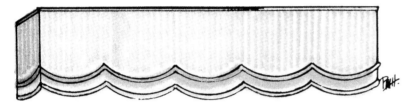

Cornice Box with Fabric Insert

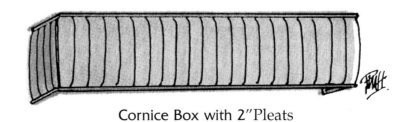

Cornice Box with 2"Pleats

103   Visual Index p.206

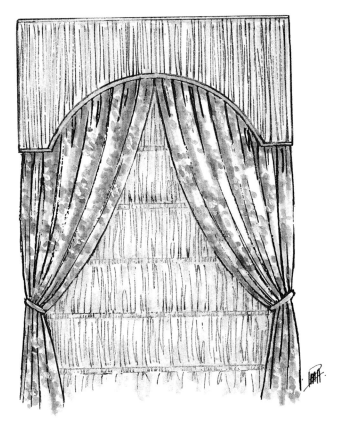

Shirred Cornice over Tie-backs

Lambrequin with Welt Edge
over Roman Shade

Shirred Lambrequin over
Pleated Drapery

Visual Index p.207

Cornice Box with Shirred
Band and Ruffled Cascade

Shaped Cornice Box with
Vertical Side Drops

Bottom Banded Cornice Box
with Matching Draperies

Visual Index p.207

Cornice Box with Gold-Leaf Heading and Ties

Cornice Box with Gathered Panels

Soft Cornice with Swags and Cascades

Arched Cornice Box with Knotted Swag

106

Visual Index p.207

Cornice Box Shapes

Visual Index p.207

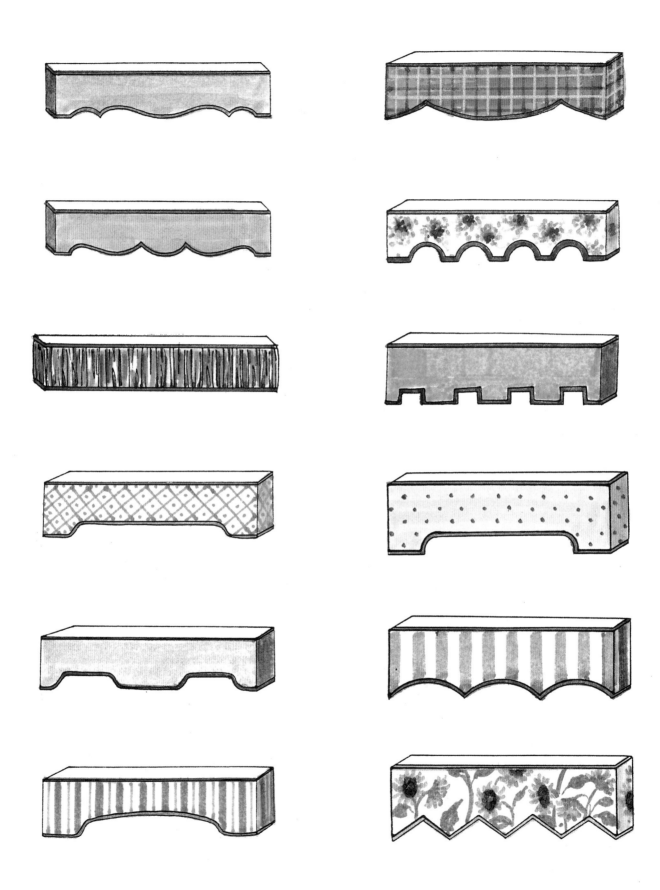

Visual Index p.208

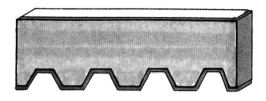

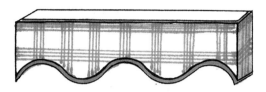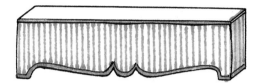

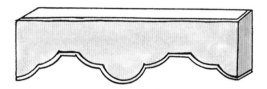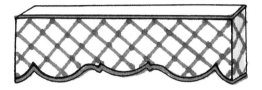

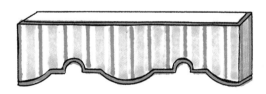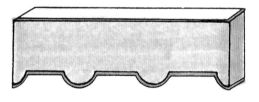

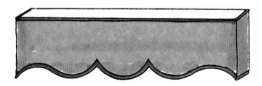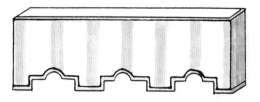

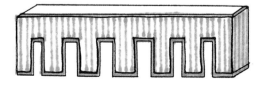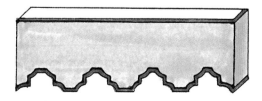

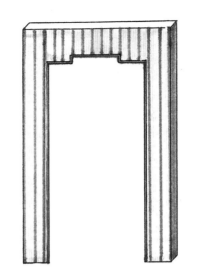

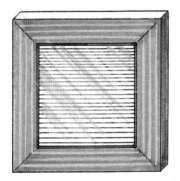

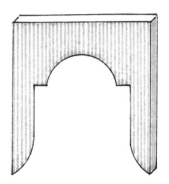

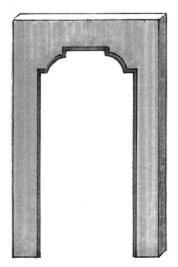

Visual Index p.208

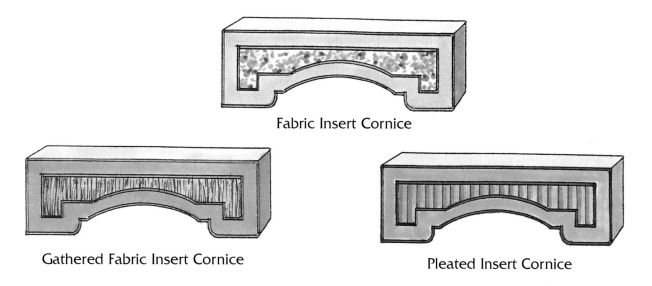

Fabric Insert Cornice

Gathered Fabric Insert Cornice

Pleated Insert Cornice

General Information

The cornices are padded with polyester fiberfill and constructed of wood.

Non-directional and solid fabrics should be railroaded to eliminate seams. Matching welting is standard on all cornices and is applied to the top and bottom edges. Coordinatng colors for welting has a more dramatic effect.

When ordering cornices to fit tight applications (i.e. wall to wall, bay windows), be sure to measure at the elevation of this installation. "Exact outside face measurement - wall to wall installation". Allow 1" for clearnace.

Measuring:

Measure drapery rod from end bracket to end bracket and add four inches for rod clearance and cornice. 6" returns are needed when mounted over a single rod and 8" returns when mounted over a double rod.

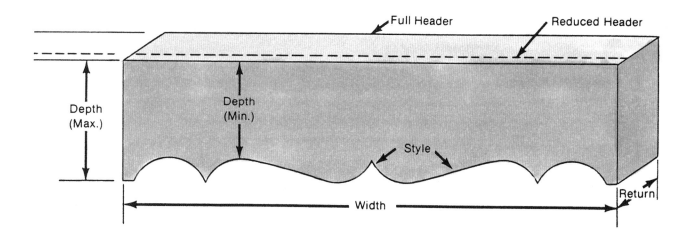

Fabric Shades

Stagecoach Shade with Ties

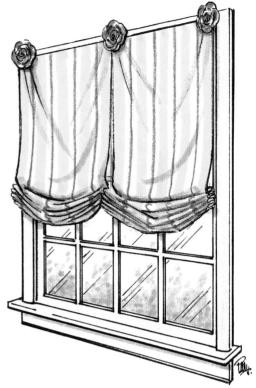

Wide Pleated Balloon Shade

Designer Cloud Shade

Wide Cloud, Shade

Visual Index p.208

Tiered Cloud Shade

Cloud Shade with Ruffled Bottom

Arched Top Cloud Shade

Bottom Arched Balloon Shade

Visual Index p.209

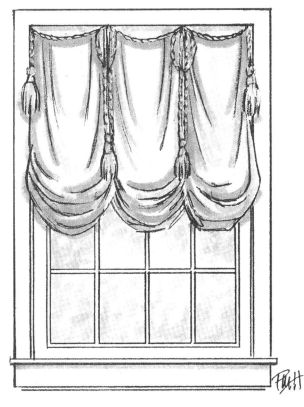

Balloon Shade with Rope Tassels

Suspender Balloon Shade

Double Rod Pocket Cloud Shade
with Bottom Ruffle

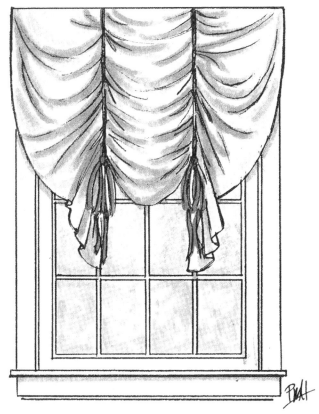

Specialty Soft Shade

Visual Index p.209

Cloud Shade with Bows at Top

Cloud Shade gathered on a pole
with ruffled upper edge

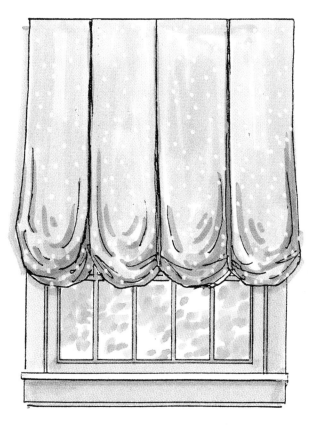

Balloon Shade

Balloon Shade with Shirred
Cornice Box

Visual Index p.209

Cloud Shade Gathered on a Pole
with Ruffle at the Top

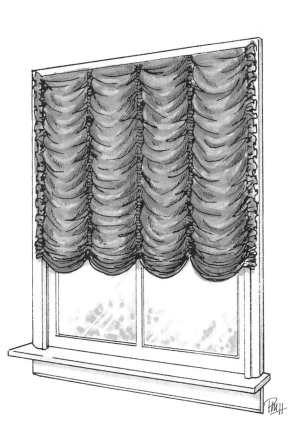

Triple Fullness Fabric in Softly Scalloped
Panels Distinguish the Austrian Shade

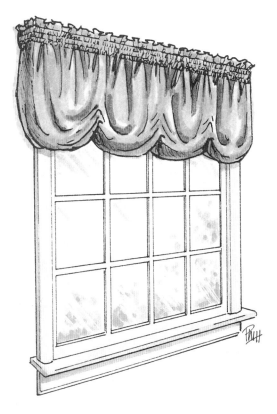

Cloud Shade with 4" Shirring
at Top to Give a Smocked Look

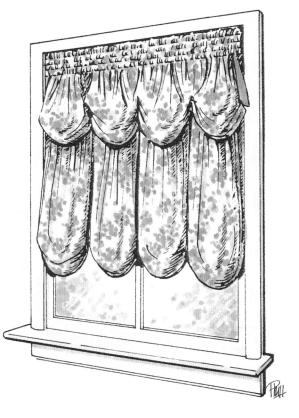

Shirred Cloud Shade with Matching Valance

Visual Index p.209

Inverted Pleats and a Pouffed Bottom Edge
Characterize the Elegant Balloon Shade

Pleated Balloon Shade with
Matching Valance

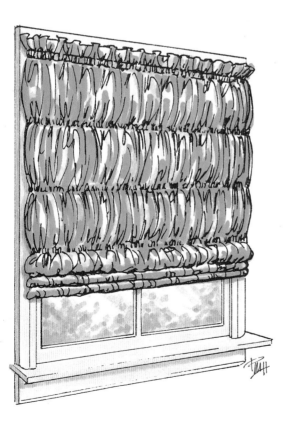

Fabric Gathered Triple Fullness on Horizontal
Rods for a Full, but Tailored Look

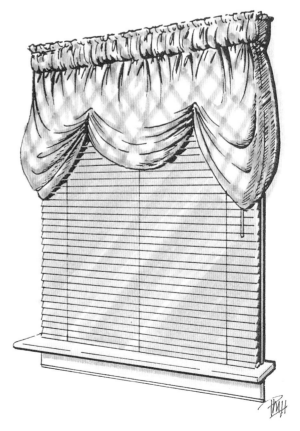

Rod Pocket Swagged Balloon Shade
over Mini Blind

Visual Index p.210

The Dramatic Accordion Look is
Created by Rows of Mini-pleats

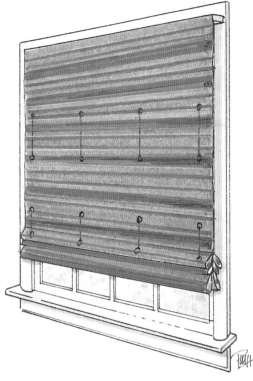

Brass Grommets and Front Cording Give
a Nautical Look to this Shade

A Flat, Simple Roman Shade that Draws
Up into Graceful Folds when Raised

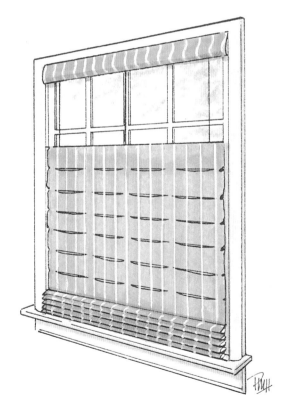

A Cord at Each Edge Gives Needed
Support to this Bottom-up Shade

Visual Index p.210

Distinctive Horizontal Pleating Makes this
a Very Popular and Versatile Roman Shade

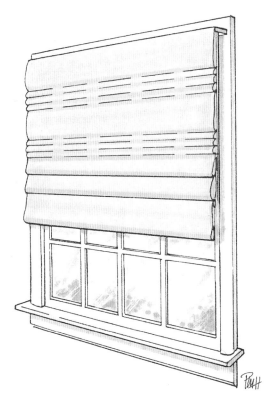

Alternate Groups of Mini-pleats with Single Panels
Gives this Blind a Striking Look all its Own

Soft Overlapping Folds Create a Cascading
Effect in this Roman Shade

Alternating Large and Small Pleats form a
Repeating Pattern on this Roman Shade

Visual Index p.210

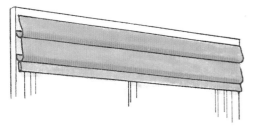

This Valance has Soft Folds
and No Returns

094B

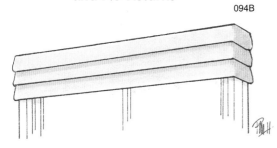

For a More Finished Look, Soft Folds Wrap
Around the Sides of this Roman Valance

Soft Mini-fold Roman Shade

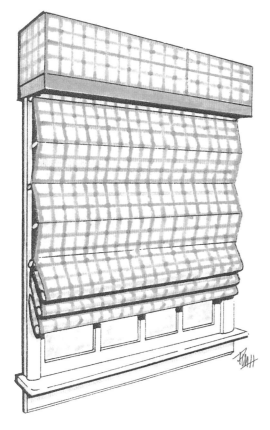

Roman Shade with Valance
Overlapping

This Very Simple Roman Shade is Flat
when Down and Draws Up in Graceful
Folds when Raised

Visual Index p.210

Fabric Shade Measuring Information

Inside Installation

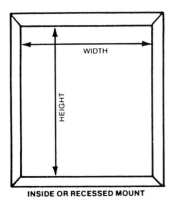

INSIDE OR RECESSED MOUNT

Outside Installation

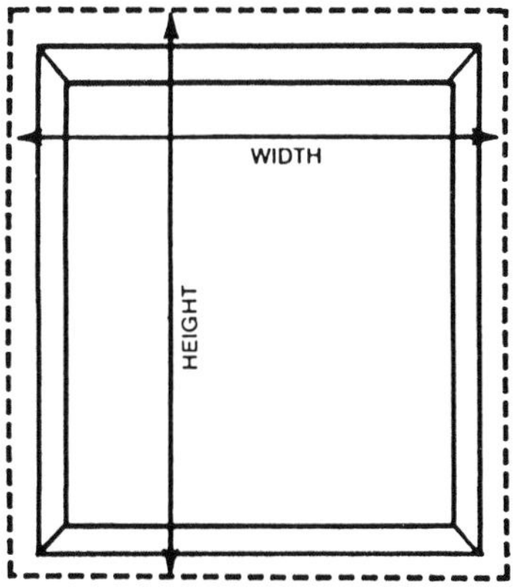

OUTSIDE OR WALL MOUNT

A. Width: Measure width of window at the top, center and bottom of window, and use narrowest measurement when ordering. Specify on order form if inside clearance has been made. If no clearance has been allowed factory will deduct ¼" from overall width.

B. Length: Measure height of window from top of opening to top of sill, no allowance is made for length.

A. Width: Measure exact width of area to be covered. It is recommended that shades extend past actual window opening by 2" on each side. Furnish finished shade width, no allowances will be made.

B. Length: Measure length of area to be covered, allowing a minimum of 2½" at top of window to accomodate headerboard and brackets. (At this time you may want to take into consideration stackage of shades and allow for this in your length measurement.) Furnish finished shade length, no allowance will be made.

ALL INSTALLATIONS

A. Specify right or left cord position. If no cord position is indicated, cords will be corded to right hand side.

B. Specify cord length (length of cord needed for easy reach, when shade is completely down). If no specification is made, cord length will be approximately ⅓ length of shade.

C. For Pole Cloud, Cloud and Balloon shades, specify if length given is high or low point of pouff.

Square Footage Chart

SHADE LENGTH in inches	SHADE WIDTH in inches																				
	24	30	36	42	48	54	60	66	72	78	84	90	96	102	108	114	120	126	132	138	144
30	10	10	10	10	10	11¼	12½	13¾	15	16¼	17½	18¾	20	21¼	22½	23¾	25	26¼	27½	28¾	30
36	10	10	10	10½	12	13½	15	16½	18	19½	21	22½	24	25½	27	28½	30	31½	33	34½	36
42	10	10	10½	12¼	14	15¾	17½	19¼	21	22¾	24½	26¼	28	29¾	31½	33¼	35	36¾	38½	40¼	42
48	10	10	12	14	16	18	20	22	24	26	28	30	32	34	36	38	40	42	44	46	48
54	10	11¼	13½	15¾	18	20¼	22½	24¾	27	29¼	31½	33¾	36	38¼	40½	42¾	45	47¼	49½	51¾	54
60	10	12½	15	17½	20	22½	25	27½	30	32½	35	37½	40	42½	45	47½	50	52½	55	57½	60
66	11	13¾	16½	19¼	22	24¾	27½	30¼	33	35¾	38½	41¼	44	46¾	49½	52¼	55	57¾	60½	63¼	66
72	12	15	18	21	24	27	30	33	36	39	42	45	48	51	54	57	60	63	66	69	72
78	13	16¼	19½	22¾	26	29¼	32½	35¾	39	42¼	45½	48¾	52	55¼	58½	61¾	65	68¼	71½	74¾	78
84	14	17½	21	24½	28	31½	35	38½	42	45½	49	52½	56	59½	63	66½	70	73½	77	80½	84
90	15	18¾	22½	26¼	30	33¾	37½	41¼	45	48¾	52½	56¼	60	63¾	67½	71¼	75	78¾	82½	86¼	90
96	16	20	24	28	32	36	40	44	48	52	56	60	64	68	72	76	80	84	88	92	96
102	17	21¼	25½	29¾	34	38¼	42½	46¾	51	55¼	59½	63¾	68	72¼	76½	80¾	85	89¼	93½	97¾	102
108	18	22½	27	31½	36	40½	45	49½	54	58½	63	67½	72	76½	81	85½	90	94½	99	103½	108
114	19	23¾	28½	33¼	38	42¾	47½	52¼	57	61¾	66½	71¼	76	80¾	85½	90¼	95	99¾	104½	109¼	114
120	20	25	30	35	40	45	50	55	60	65	70	75	80	85	90	95	100	105	110	115	120
126	21	26¼	31½	36¾	42	47¼	52½	57¾	63	68¼	73½	78¾	84	89¼	94½	99¾	105	110¼	115½	120¾	126
132	22	27½	33	38½	44	49½	55	60½	66	71½	77	82½	88	93½	99	104½	110	115½	121	126½	132
138	23	28¾	34½	40¼	46	51¾	57½	63¼	69	74¾	80½	86¼	92	97¾	103½	109¼	115	120¾	126½	132¼	138
144	24	30	36	42	48	54	60	66	72	78	84	90	96	102	108	114	120	126	132	138	144

Curtains

Tabbed Curtain over Shutters

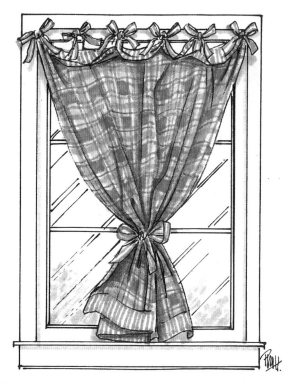

Tabbed Curtain gathered in Middle

Chevron Valance over Cafe Curtains

Curtain on Dec. Rod with Holdback

Visual Index p.211

Sheer Lace Tied-back Curtains
with Gathered Valance

Shirred Cafe Curtain on High Rod

Cafe Curtains with French Pleated
Tops on Rings

Scalloped Valance over
Cafe Curtains

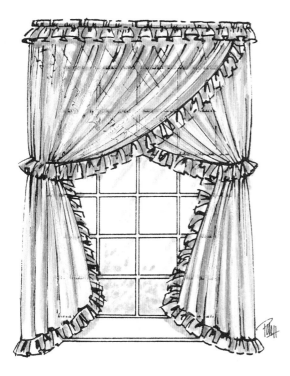

Priscilla Curtains with Ruffles

Valance on Brass Dec. Rod over
Tied-back Curtains with Ruffles

Rod Top Curtains with High Ties
and Large Ruffles

Priscilla Curtains with Rod Pocket Top

Visual Index p.211

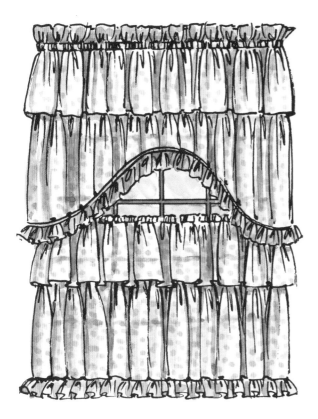

Cafe Curtains with Arched Top & Valance

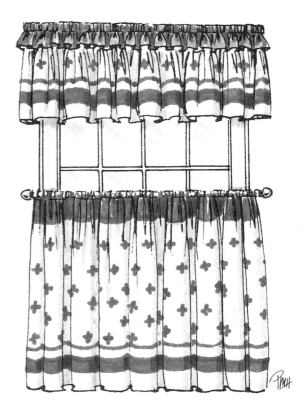

Cafe Curtains on Brass Rod with
Gathered Valance

Traditional Swag with Mini Blind

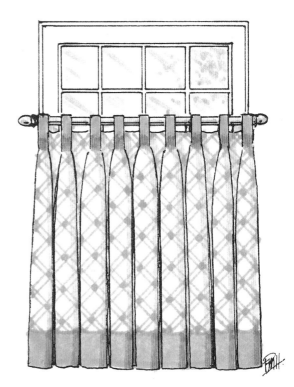

Pleated Tab Top Cafe Curtains
on Brass Rod

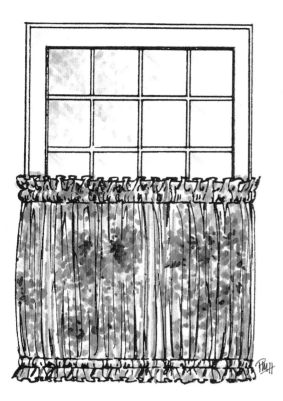

Cafe Curtains Shirred Top-to-Bottom
Between Two Rods

Tied-back Curtains Gathered on Rod

Drapery Gathered on a Dec. Rod and
Tied-back with Large Bows

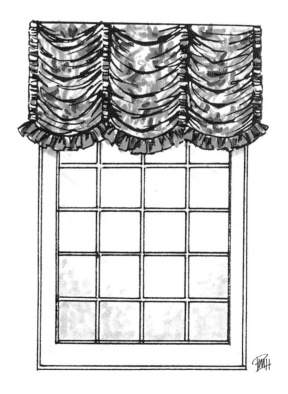

Austrian Shade with Ruffles

Visual Index p.212

Hourglass Rod Pocket

Cloud Valance with Rod Pocket Top
and Bottom Drapery

Diamond Rod Pocket

Slant Top Rod Pocket

127

Visual Index p.212

Bow-tied Ruffled Tie-backs

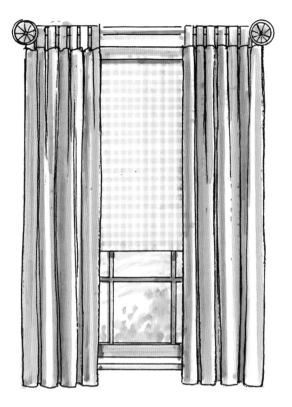

Tab-top Curtains on Dec. Rod

Ruffled Tie-backs over Balloon Shade

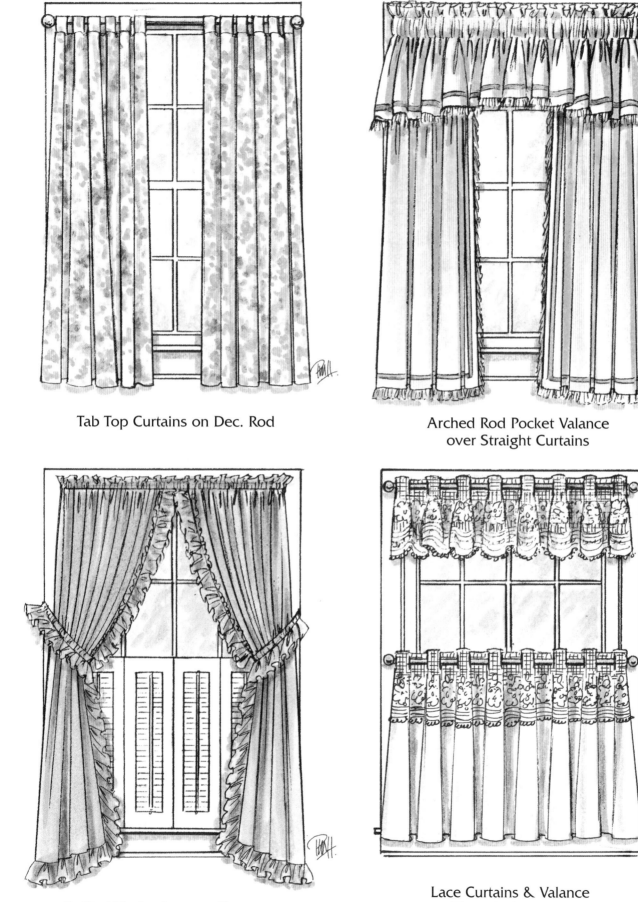

Tab Top Curtains on Dec. Rod

Arched Rod Pocket Valance
over Straight Curtains

Ruffled Tie-backs over Shutters

Lace Curtains & Valance
Threaded on Rod

129

Visual Index p.212

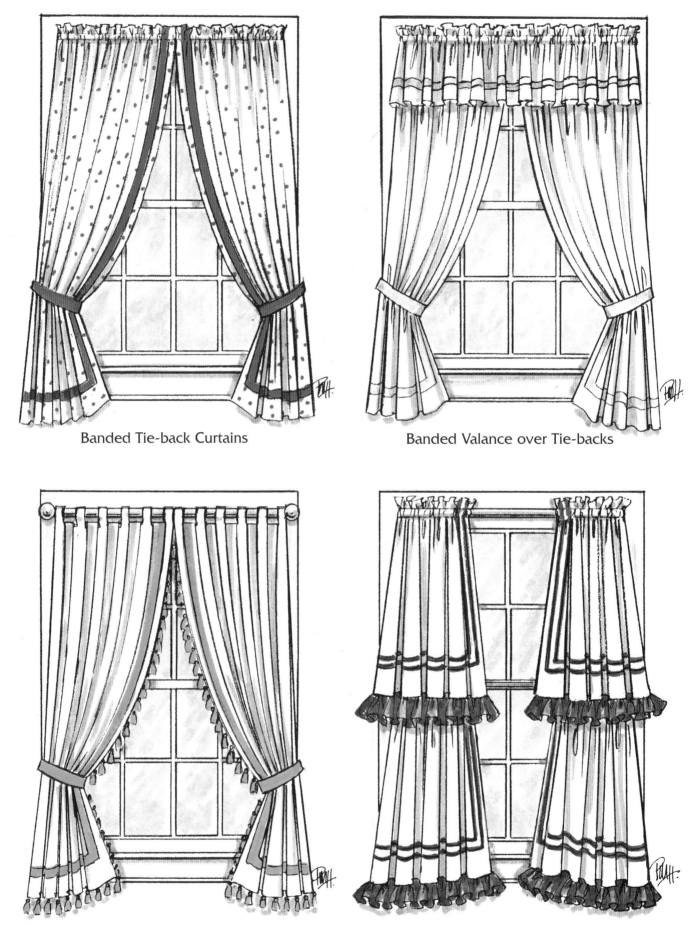

Banded Tie-back Curtains

Banded Valance over Tie-backs

Tab Top Banded Curtains Tied-back

Tiered Curtains with Ribbon Banding

130

Visual Index p.213

Box Pleated with Tab Heading

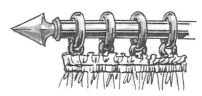

Gathered Heading with Rings

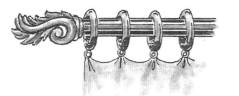

Scalloped Heading with Sewn on Rings

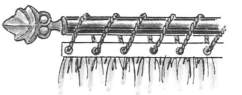

Grommet Heading with Rope

Scalloped Heading with Ties

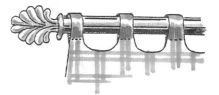

Scalloped & Tabbed Heading

Tab-tied Curtains on Brass Dec. Rod

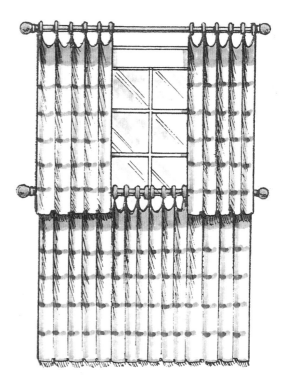

Double Cafe Curtains with Scalloped
Top on Brass Rod

Visual Index p.213

Accessories

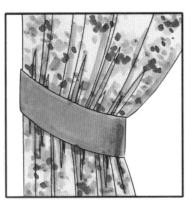

Straight Plain

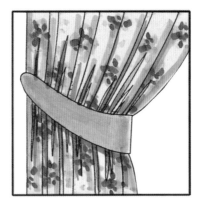

Tapered Plain

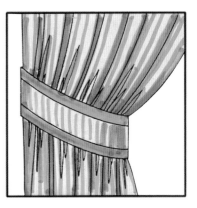

Straight with Banding

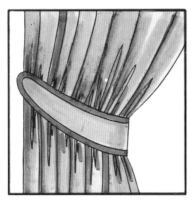

Tapered with Weld Cord

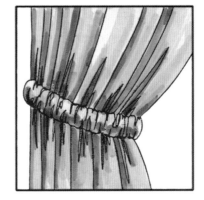

Shirred Jumbo Welt Cord

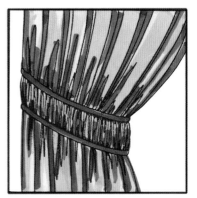

Straight Shirred with
Welt Cord

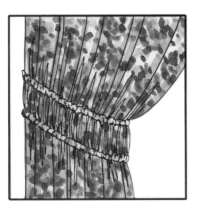

Straight Shirred

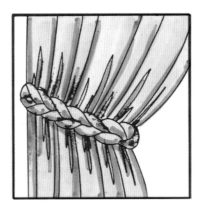

Braided

Straight with Rosette

     Visual Index p.213

Straight with Bow

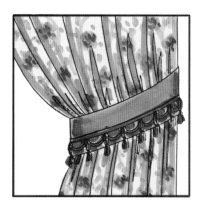

Straight with Fringe

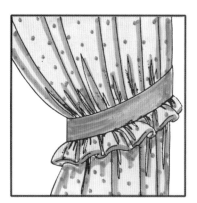

Straight with Ruffle

Ruffled

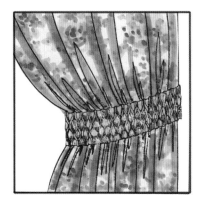

New Shirred Look

Formal Tie with Cascade

Shirred Tie with Pleat

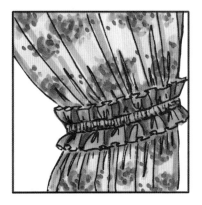

Double Ruffled Tie

Box Pleated Tie with Welt

Visual Index p.213

Throw Pillows

Turkish Corners

Knife Edge with 1/4" Welt

3" Ruffle with Welt

Shirred Welt

Heart Shaped with Ruffle

Square Knot

Round Pillow with Welt & Ruffle

Round Pillow with Plain Welt & Button

Round Pillow with Plain Welt & Button

Rope Welt on Knife Edge

Scalloped Ruffle with Welt Edge

Tasseled Corners

Visual Index p.214

Pillows and Cushions

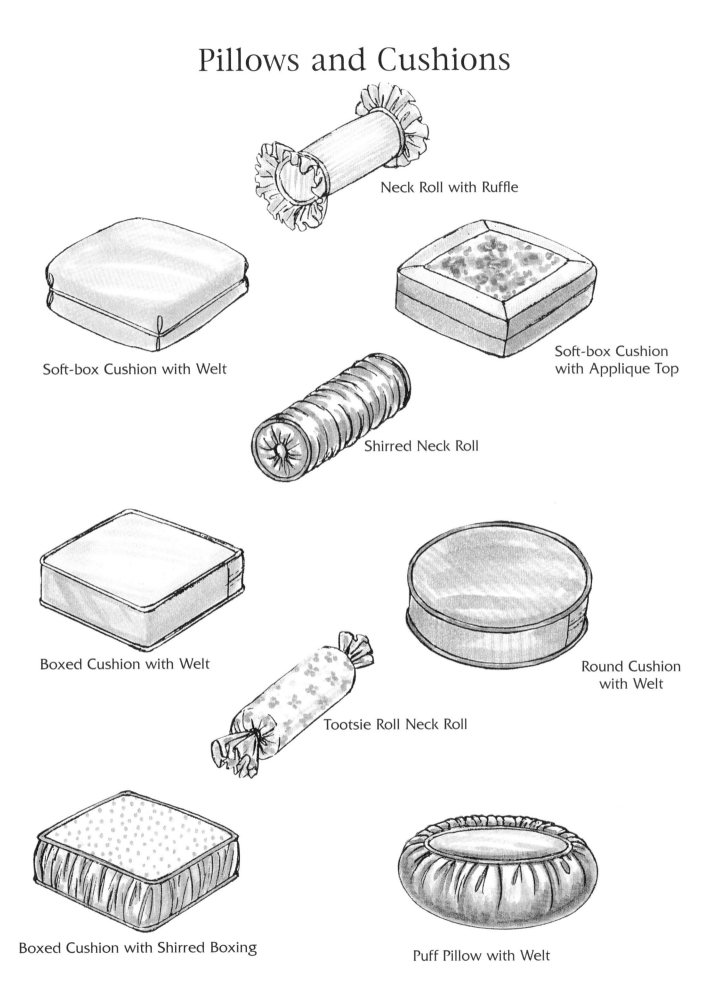

Neck Roll with Ruffle

Soft-box Cushion with Welt

Soft-box Cushion
with Applique Top

Shirred Neck Roll

Boxed Cushion with Welt

Round Cushion
with Welt

Tootsie Roll Neck Roll

Boxed Cushion with Shirred Boxing

Puff Pillow with Welt

Visual Index p.214

Accessories

Placemats

Seat Cushions

Lamp Shades

Napkins & Napkin Rings

Rosettes

Bows

Visual Index p.214

Round Ottoman

Square Ottoman

Fabric Draped Vanity Table

Slip-covered Chair

Fabric Covered Divider

Fabric Draped Through Sconces

Fabric Covered
Wastebasket

Seat Cushion

Sconce

Visual Index p.214

Round Table Covers

Ruffled Overlay & Skirt with Tassels

Round Overlay Tied with Bows

Plain Round Cover — Lined or Unlined

Plain Round Cover with Welt Edge

Lace Square over Skirt

Round Cover with Austrian Shirring

Visual Index p.215

Sunburst

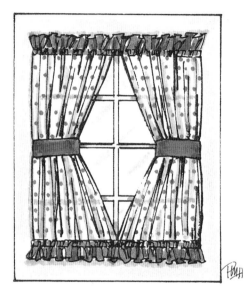

Diamond Rod Top & Bottom

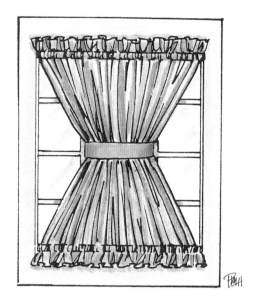

Hourglass Rod Top & Bottom

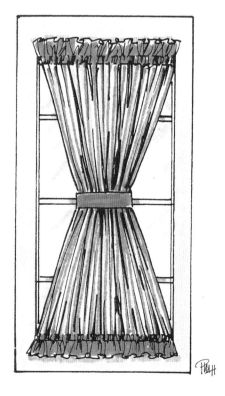

Hourglass Rod Top & Bottom

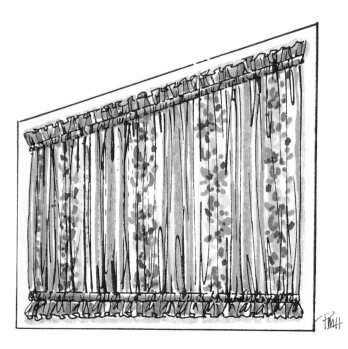

Slant Rod Top & Bottom

Bed Coverings

Various Bedspread Crowns

Rod Pocket Drapery with Dec. Rod
over Plain Bedspread

Swags & Cascades over Plain bedspread
with Upholstered Headboard

Swags & Jabots with Maltese Cross Ties
over Plain Bedspread

Visual Index p.215

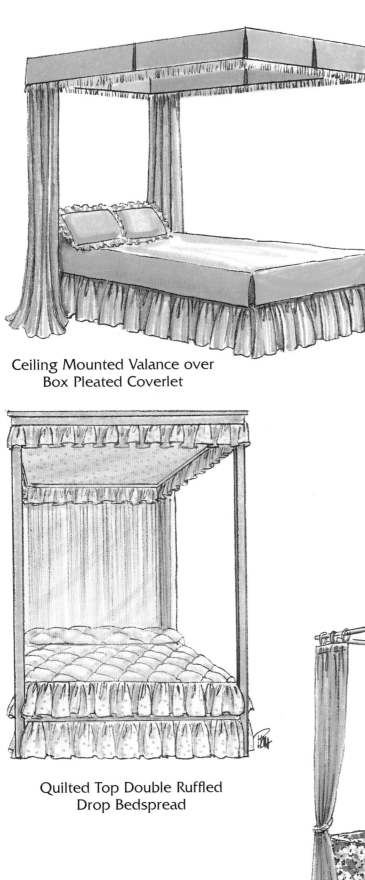

Ceiling Mounted Valance over
Box Pleated Coverlet

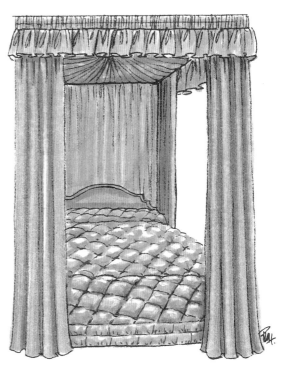

Ceiling Mounted Rod Pocket Valance
over Quilted Bedspread

Quilted Top Double Ruffled
Drop Bedspread

Plain Bedspread with
Side Panels

Visual Index p.215

Half-round Box Pleated Valance
with Draped Fabric held by Rosettes
Upholstered Headboard with Throw Spread

Fabric Draped over Decorative Pole
Coverlet with Tailored Dust Ruffle

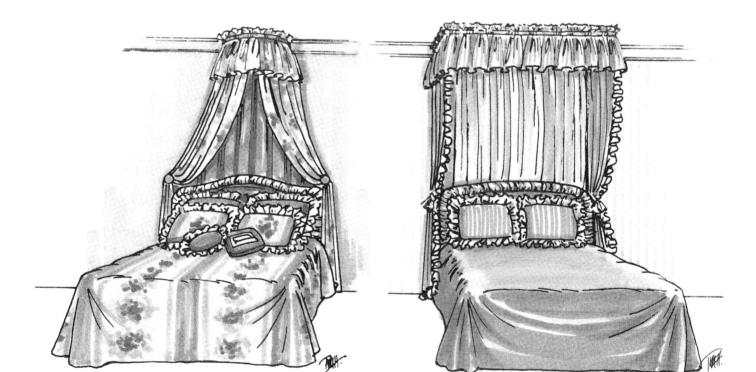

Half-round Ruffled Valance with
Fabric Draped over Hold Backs
Upholstered Headboard with Throw Spread

Rod Pocket Valance with Ruffled Tie-backs
Upholstered Headboard & Throw Spread

Visual Index p.216

Box Pleated Canopy Valance
    with Stationary Draperies

Quilted Coverlet over
    Box Pleated Dust Ruffle

Gathered Canopy Valance
Ruffled Bedspread over Gathered
    Dust Ruffle

Arched Canopy with Ruffles
Ruffled Bedspread & Dust Ruffle

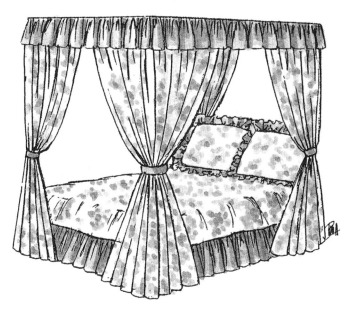

Gathered Canopy Valance over Tie-backs
Coverlet over Gathered Dust Ruffle

Visual Index p.216

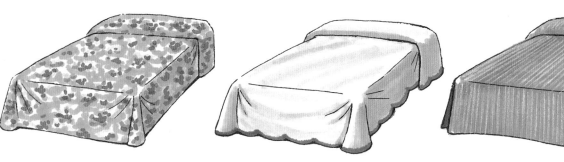

Throw Spread

Throw with Scalloped Edge

Fitted Throw

Scalloped Quilted Top
with Shirred Drop

Scalloped Quilted Top
with Double Shirred Drop

Throw with
Ruffled Bottom

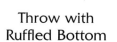
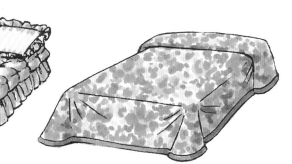

Plain Coverlet over
Shirred Dust Ruffle

Quilted Coverlet over
Shirred Dust Ruffle

Throw with 1" Welt

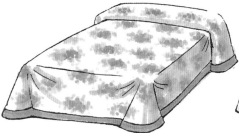

Throw with 2" Welt

Studio Couch Cover
with Bolsters

Tufted Daybed Comforter
over Shirred Dust Ruffle

Visual Index p.216

Upholstered Benches

Plain Covered Bench

Covered Scalloped Bench

Double Bench with Shirred Skirt

Plain Bench with
Upholstered Legs & Top

Pillow Shams

Sham with 3" Ruffle

Plain Sham with
1/4" Welt

Quilted Sham with
2 1/2" Flange

Plain Sham with
Double Ruffle

Sham with 1/4" Welt
and Ruffle

Double Ruffle Sham
with 1/2" Welt

Cylindrical Bolster
with Welt Trim

Wedge Bolster with
Welt Trim

Rectangular Bolster
with Welt Trim

Visual Index p.216

Yardage Schedule for Bed Coverings

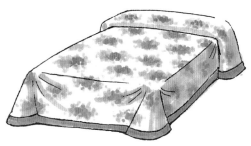

SPREADS			
	36"	48"	54"
Twin	12 yards	8 yards	8 yards
Full	12 yards	12 yards	8 yards
Queen	15 yards	12 yards	12 yards
King	15 yards	12 yards	12 yards

Additional Yardage Requirements: For Prints—Add 1 yard
Additional Yardage Optional Features:
For Reverse Sham—Add 3 yards   For Jumbo Cord—Add 2 yards

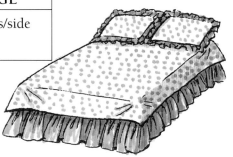

COMFORTER YARDAGE
Twin, Full, Queen— 7 yards/side
King—11 yards/side

PILLOW SHAMS
1 1/2 yards—Ruffles Add 1 1/2 yards

DUSTERS				
	36" Fabric		45" or Wider	
	Tailored	Shirred or 4" Box Pleat	Tailored	Shirred or 4" Box Pleat
Twin	3 3/4 yards	8 1/2 yards	2 3/4 yards	6 1/2 yards
Full	3 3/4 yards	8 1/2 yards	2 3/4 yards	7 yards
Queen	4 1/2 yards	10 yards	3 yards	7 1/2 yards
King	4 1/2 yards	10 yards	3 yards	7 1/2 yards

BOLSTERS			
	36"	45"	54"
36"	1 1/2 yards	1 1/2 yards	1 yard
39"	2 yards	1 1/2 yards	1 yard
60"	2 yards	2 yards	2 yards
72"	2 1/2 yards	2 yards	2 yards

Add 1 Repeat of Pattern for Prints

GENERAL INFORMATION		
Bedspreads are made to fit the following standard bed sizes:		Standard Drops:
Twin	39 x 75	Bedspreads 21"
Full	54 x 75	Coverlets 12"
Queen	60 x 80	Dusters 14"
King	72 x 84	Pillow Tuck 15"

Dust Ruffles

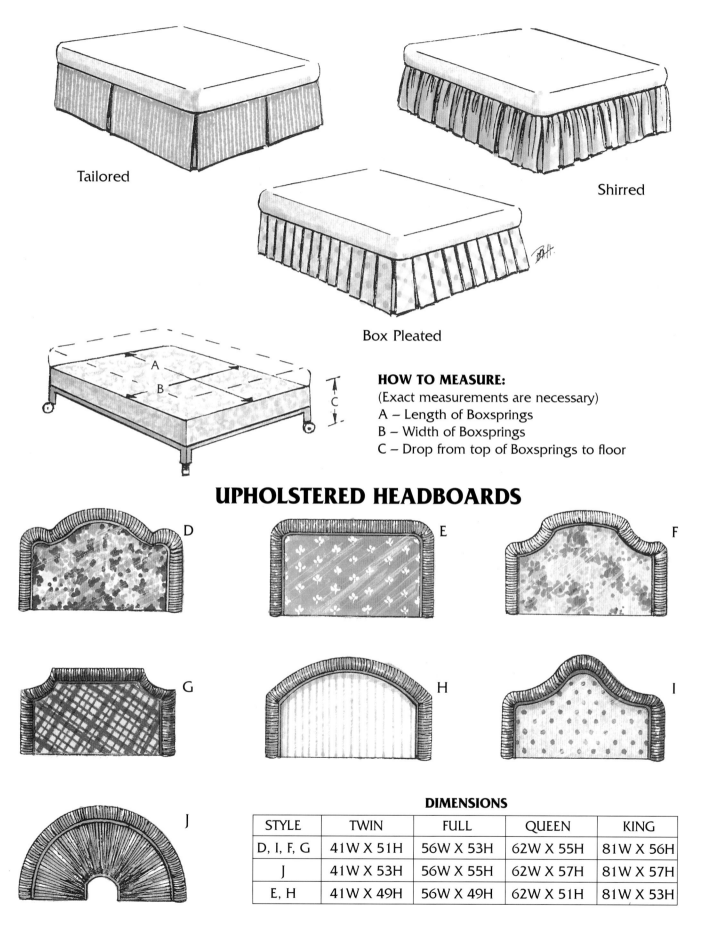

Tailored

Shirred

Box Pleated

HOW TO MEASURE:
(Exact measurements are necessary)
A – Length of Boxsprings
B – Width of Boxsprings
C – Drop from top of Boxsprings to floor

UPHOLSTERED HEADBOARDS

D

E

F

G

H

I

J

DIMENSIONS

STYLE	TWIN	FULL	QUEEN	KING
D, I, F, G	41W X 51H	56W X 53H	62W X 55H	81W X 56H
J	41W X 53H	56W X 55H	62W X 57H	81W X 57H
E, H	41W X 49H	56W X 49H	62W X 51H	81W X 53H

Visual Index p.217

Blinds and Shutters

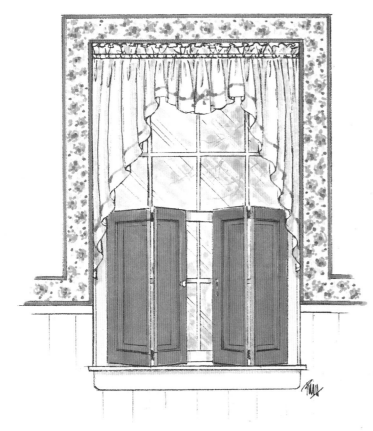

Rod Pocket Valance over Solid Wood Shutters

Louvered & Solid Shutters with Valance

Fabric Insert Shutters

Draperies over Traditional Shutters

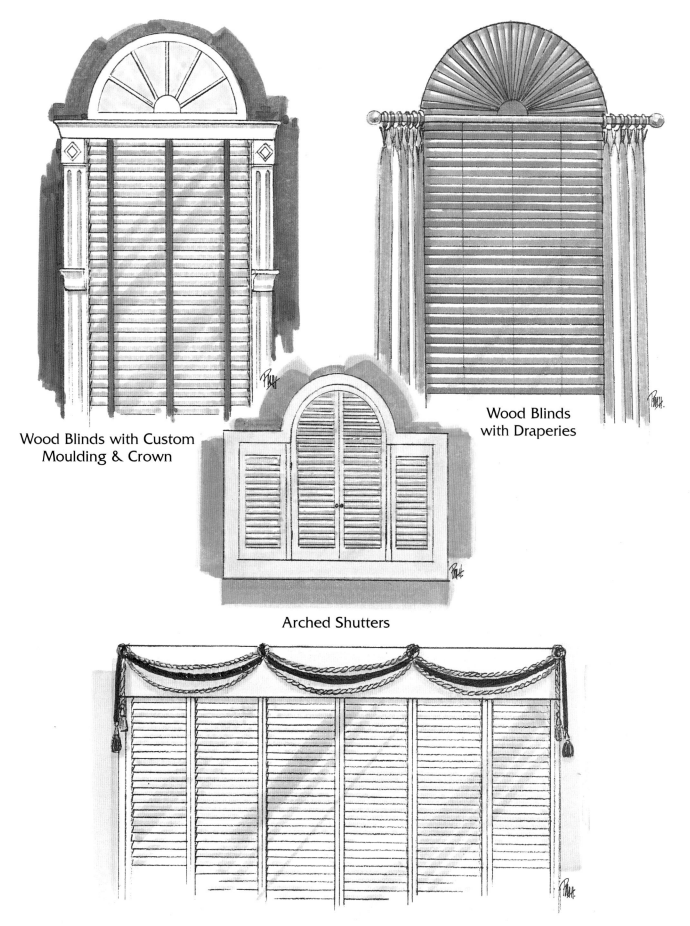

Wood Blinds with Custom
Moulding & Crown

Wood Blinds
with Draperies

Arched Shutters

Cornice Box with Rope & Tassels over Shutters

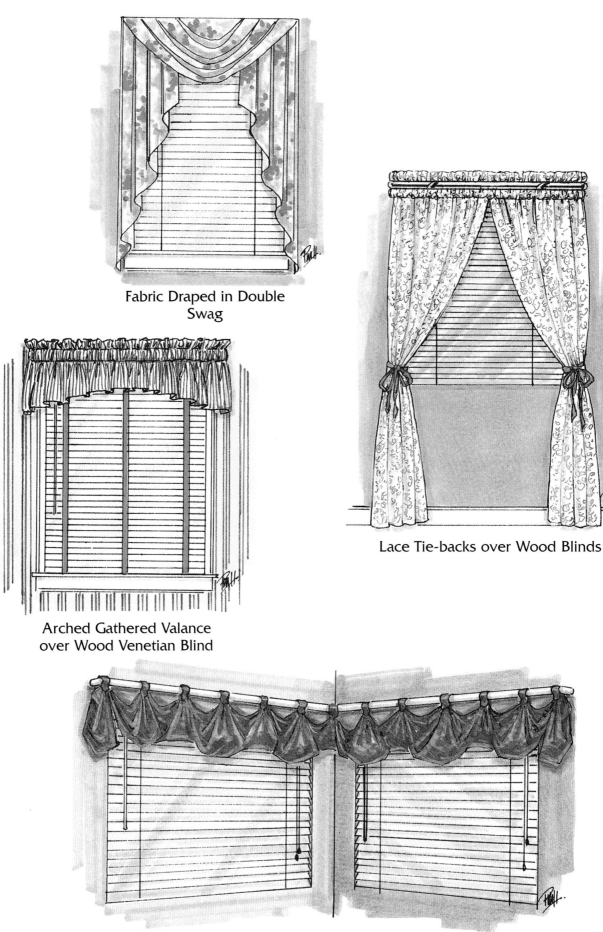

Fabric Draped in Double
Swag

Lace Tie-backs over Wood Blinds

Arched Gathered Valance
over Wood Venetian Blind

Tabbed Valance on Dec. Rod
over Wood Blind

Visual Index p.217

Swag and Jabots
over Half Shutters

Shirred Valance with Ruffle over
Gathered Side Draperies and Wood Blind

Bishop Sleeve Arched Valance
over Plantation Shutters

Cloud Valance over Half Shutters

151 Visual Index p.218

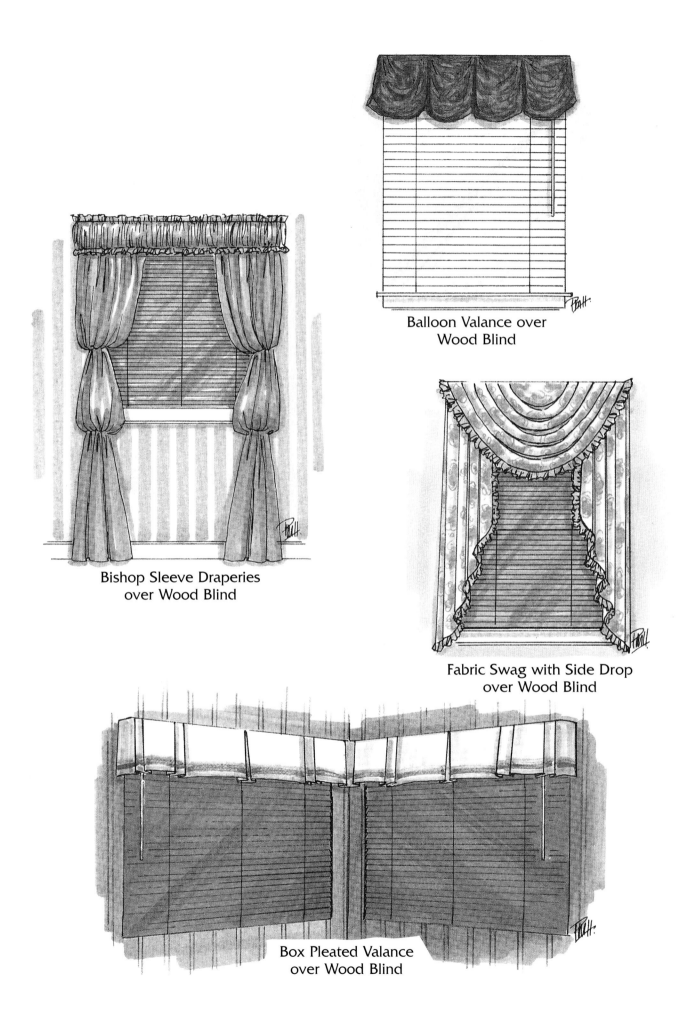

Balloon Valance over
Wood Blind

Bishop Sleeve Draperies
over Wood Blind

Fabric Swag with Side Drop
over Wood Blind

Box Pleated Valance
over Wood Blind

Visual Index p.218

Ruffled Swags over Cafe Shutters

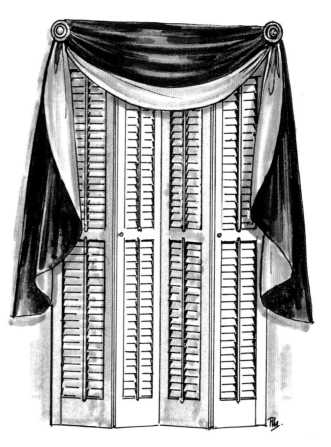

Two-tone Swag over Full Shutters

Shutter with Shirred Fabric Insert

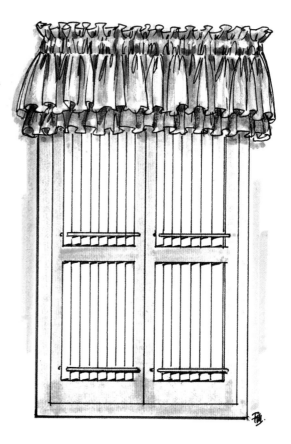

Gathered Valance over
Louvered Shutters

Visual Index p.218

Cornice Box over White Wood
Blinds with Wide Tapes

Sunburst Shutter over French Door Shutters

Leaded Glass over Wide Blade Shutters

1" Wood Blind in Natural Finish
with Cloud Valance

Visual Index p.218

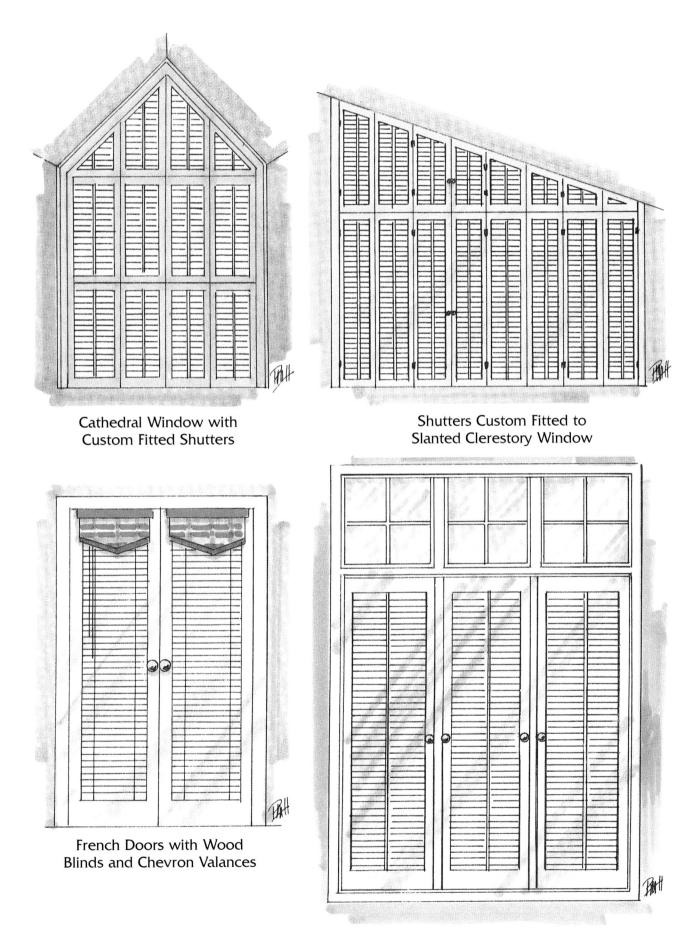

Cathedral Window with
Custom Fitted Shutters

Shutters Custom Fitted to
Slanted Clerestory Window

French Doors with Wood
Blinds and Chevron Valances

Traditional Shutters
on Tall Window

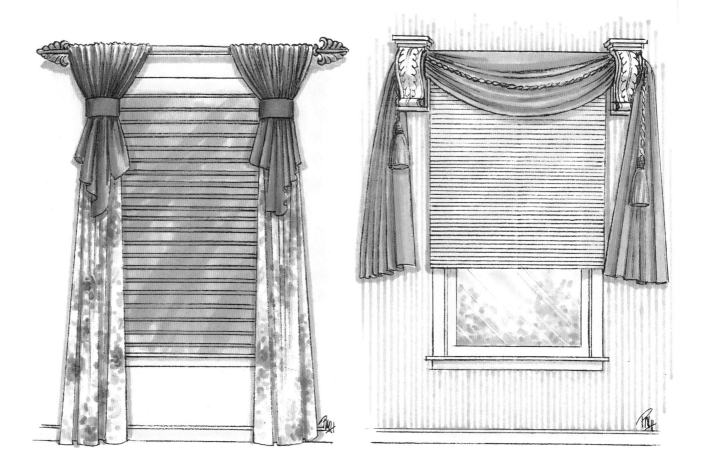

Drapery Folded over Dec. Rod over
Pleated Shade

Fabric Draped over Pleated Shade

Fabric Draped over Pleated Shade

Visual Index p.219

Cloud Valance over Mini Blind

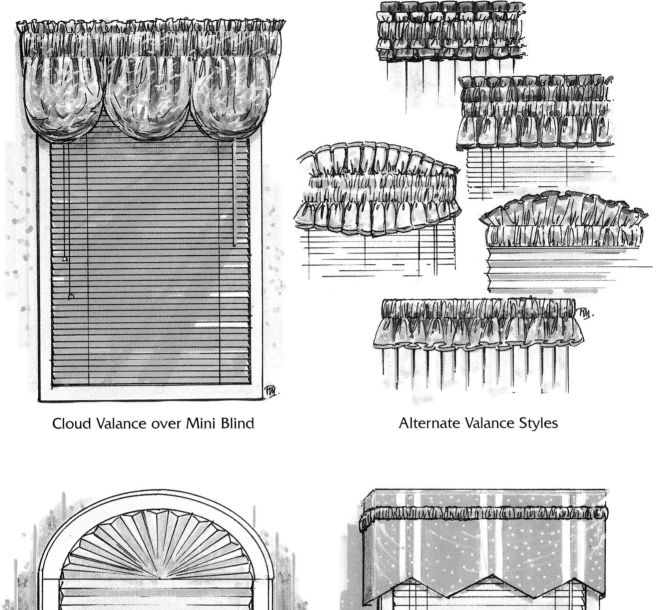

Alternate Valance Styles

Pleated Shade with Arched
Pleated Shade at Top

Unique Geometric Valance over Mini Blind

Gathered Valance with Bows over Shade
with Appliqued Bottom

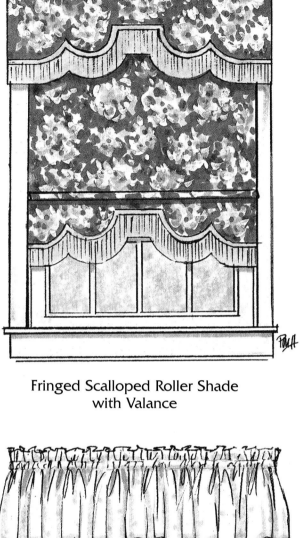

Fringed Scalloped Roller Shade
with Valance

Banded Roller Shade with Valance

Rod Pocket Valance over Roller Shade

158

Visual Index p.219

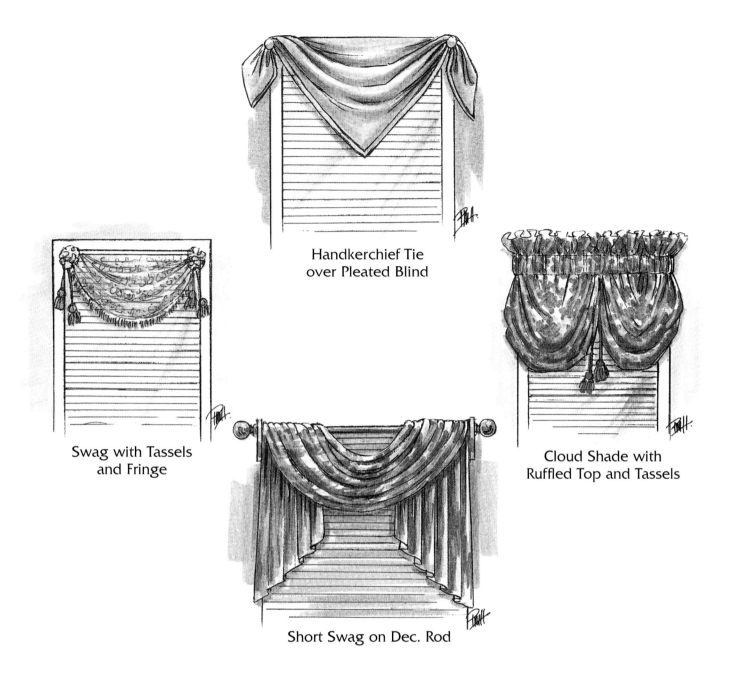

Handkerchief Tie
over Pleated Blind

Swag with Tassels
and Fringe

Cloud Shade with
Ruffled Top and Tassels

Short Swag on Dec. Rod

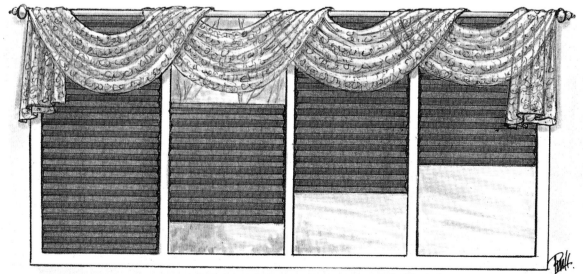

Multiple Lace Fabric Swags on Dec. Rod

Visual Index p.220

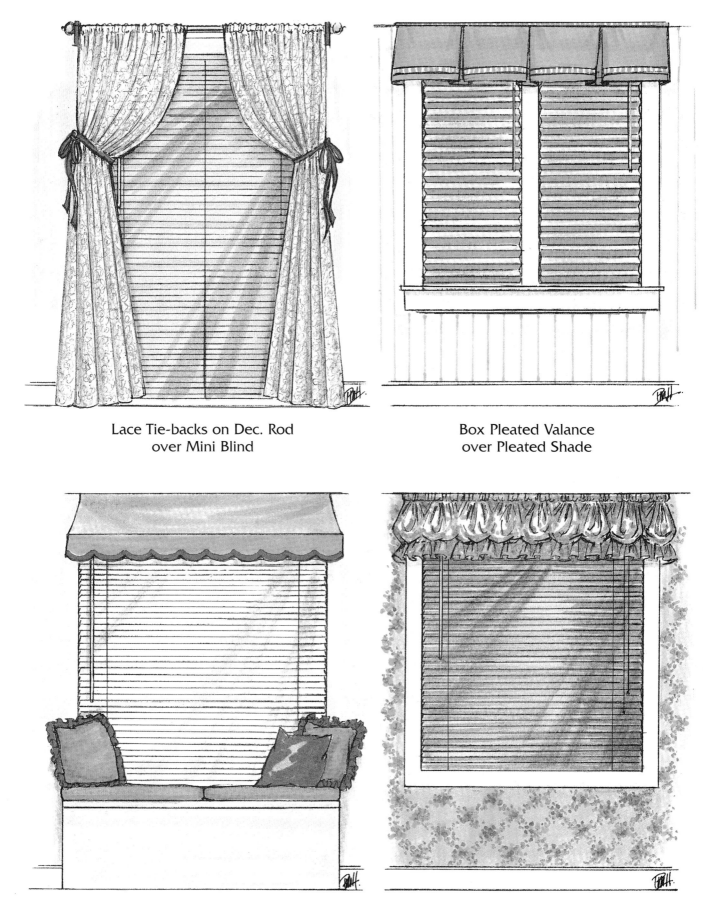

Lace Tie-backs on Dec. Rod
over Mini Blind

Box Pleated Valance
over Pleated Shade

Scalloped Awning Valance
over Mini Blind

Full Gathered Valance
on Double Rods

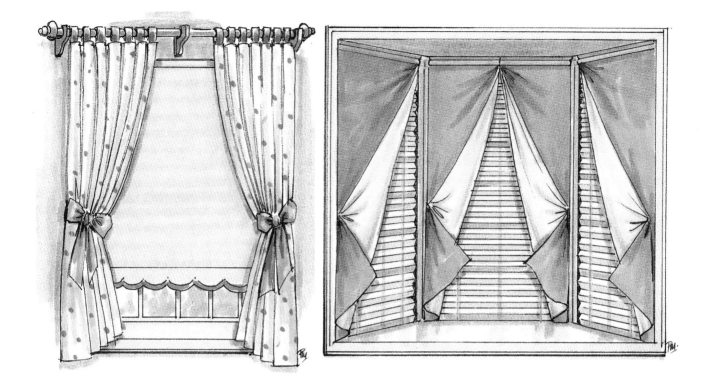

Tab Curtains Tied-back
over Roller Shade

Flat Panels Pulled Back over Pleated Shades

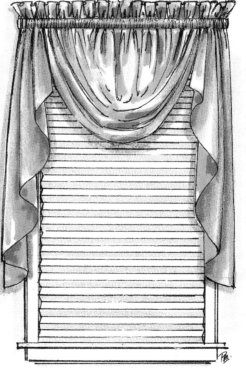

Puffed and Ruffled Valance
over Pleated Shade

Gathered Swag and Cascade
over Pleated Shade

Visual Index p.220

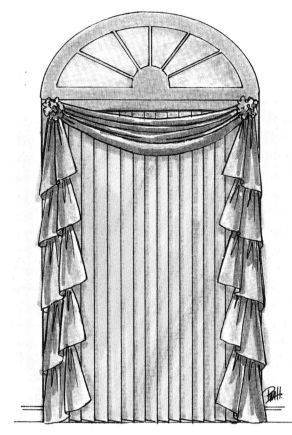

Swag with Ruffled Side Drops
over Vertical Blinds

Floor Length Fabric Swagged on
Shirred Rod over Vertical Blinds

Bay Window with Bishop Sleeve
effect over Vertical Blinds

Visual Index p.220

Simple Shirred Cornice over Vertical Blinds

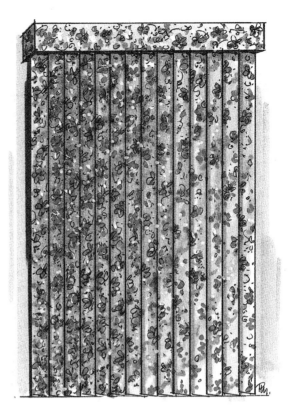

Fabric or Wallpaper Inserts

Double Gathered Cornice over Vertical Blinds

Vertical Blinds with Stagecoach Valance

Visual Index p.221

Slant-top Vertical Blinds

Vertical Blinds with Cornice Top

Verticals are a great Solution to Bay Windows

Shirred Cloud Valance Adds
Softness to Vertical Blinds

Visual Index p.221

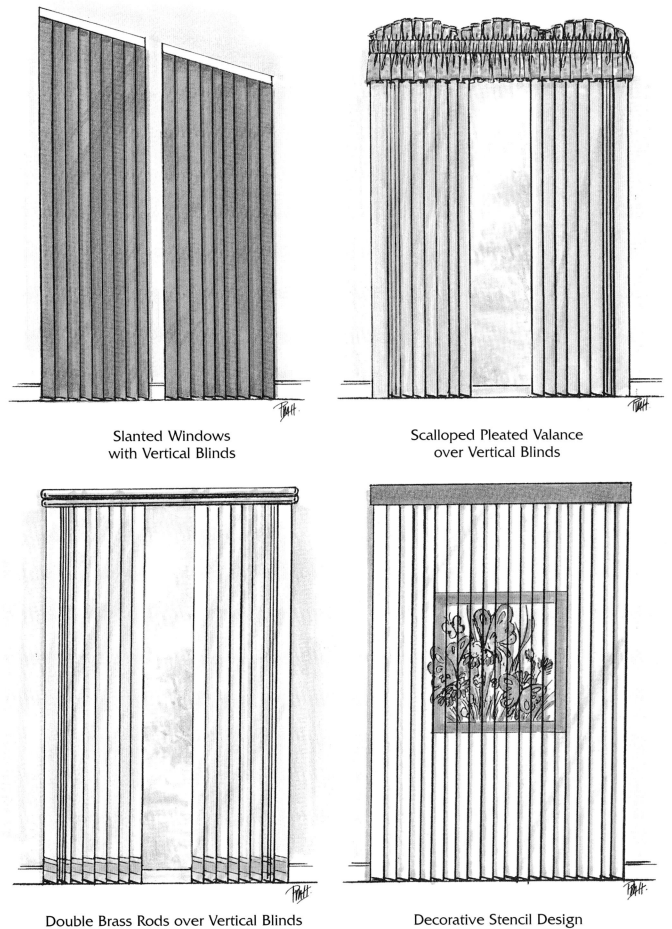

Slanted Windows
with Vertical Blinds

Scalloped Pleated Valance
over Vertical Blinds

Double Brass Rods over Vertical Blinds
with Brass Trim at Bottom

Decorative Stencil Design
on Vertical Blinds

165

Visual Index p.221

Windows with a challenge

Door with Window & Sidelights

SOLUTION 1

SOLUTION 2

Corner Gliding Windows with Structural Beam on Top

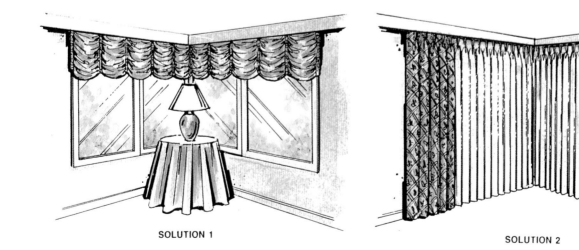

SOLUTION 1

SOLUTION 2

Visual Index p.221

Corner Windows

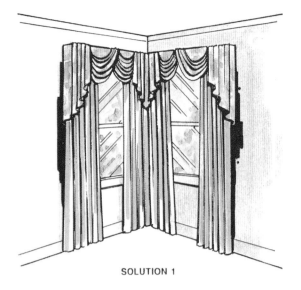

SOLUTION 1

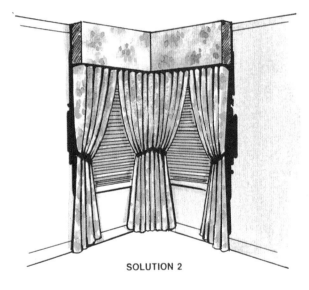

SOLUTION 2

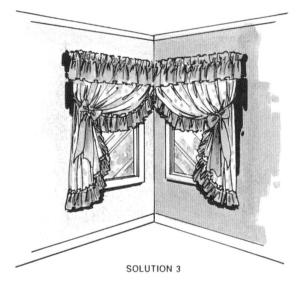

SOLUTION 3

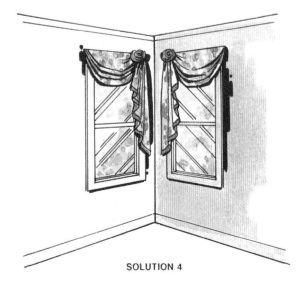

SOLUTION 4

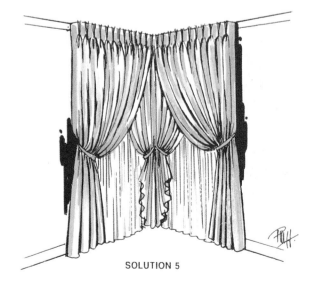

SOLUTION 5

Visual Index p.222

Air Conditioner in a Double-Hung Window

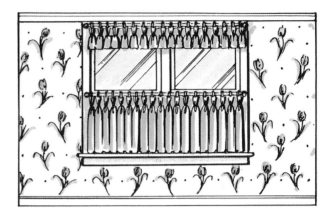

SOLUTION 1

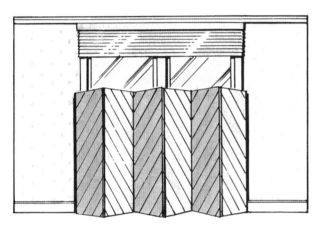

SOLUTION 2

Sliding Glass Doors & Cathedral Windows

SOLUTION 1

SOLUTION 2

168

Visual Index p.222

SOLUTION 3

SOLUTION 4

SOLUTION 5

SOLUTION 6

Clerestory Windows

SOLUTION 1

169

Visual Index p.222

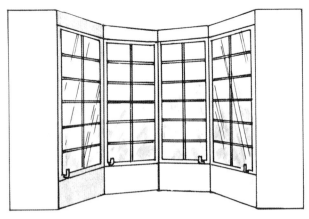

Bay with Casement Windows

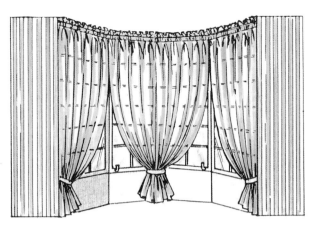

SOLUTION 1

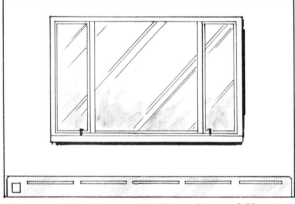

SOLUTION 2

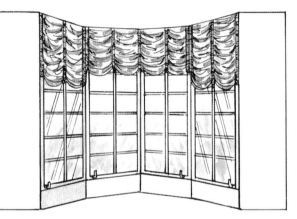

SOLUTION 3

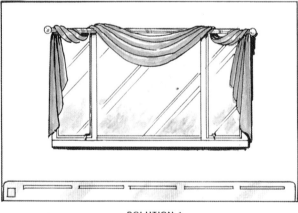

Picture Window with Baseboard Heater

SOLUTION 1

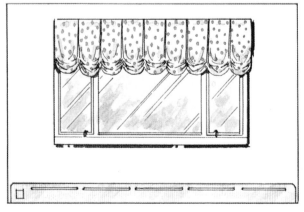

SOLUTION 2

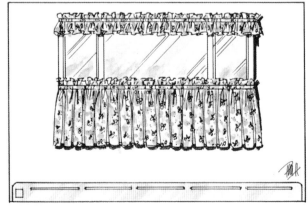

SOLUTION 3

Visual Index p.222

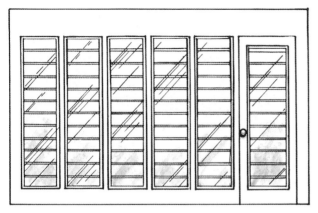

Jalousie Windows & Doors

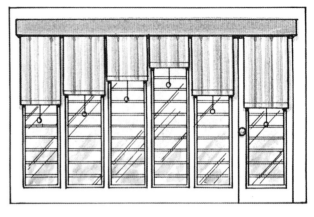

SOLUTION 1

SOLUTION 2

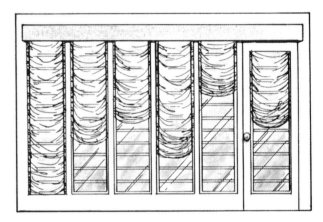

SOLUTION 3

French Doors

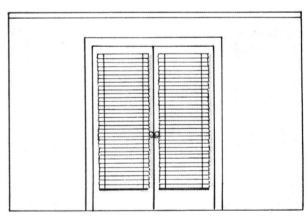

SOLUTION 1

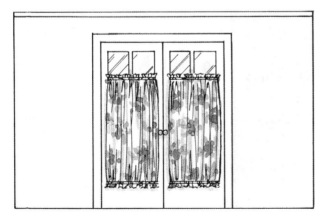

SOLUTION 2

SOLUTION 3

Visual Index p.223

Triple Double-Hung Windows

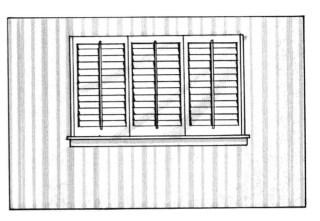

SOLUTION 1

SOLUTION 2

SOLUTION 3

Bay with Double-Hung Windows

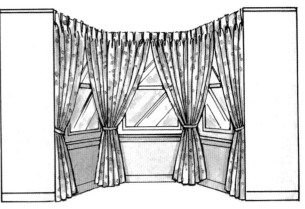

SOLUTION 1

SOLUTION 2

SOLUTION 3

Visual Index p.223

Arched Top Windows

SOLUTION 1

SOLUTION 2

SOLUTION 3

SOLUTION 4

SOLUTION 5

Visual Index p.223

Glossary of Decorating Terms

A

"A" Frame Window - Very contemporary house structures sometimes form an "A" shape. When draperies are used, they hang from the crossbeam of the "A," or they can be fabricated and installed to conform to the shape of the window.

A La Duchesse - A type of bed supported with a canopy suspension from the ceiling rather than posts. It is also know as an angel bed.

Accordion Pleat - Single large pleats which are often used as a method of fan folding in pleated draperies before installing, or can be used in contract draperies by snapping onto channel slides.

Allowance - A customary variation from an "exact" measurement, taken for the purpose of anticipated needs.

Appliqué - The application of a second, decorated layer of fabric onto a base piece of cloth.

Apron - A piece of wood trim beneath the windowsill.

Architectural Rodding - Used for contract draperies, a sturdy sleek or traverse channel.

Architrave - The molding around an arch, or wooden surrounding to a window or door frame.

Art Deco - A modern, historical design period, which dates from 1909 to 1939.

Art Glass - Glass which is cut at an angle (other than right), stained and etched, and used for hard window treatments.

Art Nouveau - An historical design movement of the Victorian Era, dating from 1890 to 1910. The motifs are based on flowing plant forms.

Asymmetrical Balance - A type of design in which the entire arrangement has a balance, but each side of a central point is different.

Austrian Shade - A shade having ruche down the whole side length, creating billows when the shade is raised.

Automated Exterior Rolling Shutters - A treatment used for insulation and privacy purposes, in which the exterior of a window has metal panels, which roll down mechanically over the glass.

Awning Window - A type of window which can swing out due to a hinged top.

B

Backstitch - A reverse-stitch used to keep the stitches from coming undone at the ends. Several stitches are sewn at the beginning and end of any seam.

Balloon Shade - Shades with vertical rows of horizontally gathered fabric, which can be drawn up to form strips of pleated or gathered trim.

Balloon Tie-backs - Curtains which, when tied back, form a rounded sort of cloud shape.

Bamboo Shade - A natural light softening shade, drawn by hand using a cord, and made of woven panels of split bamboo. This is also called a Bali blind.

Baroque - An elaborate interior design period dating from 1643 to 1730 in France and 1660 to 1714 in England.

Bar-Tack - A sewing machine operation of repeated stitches concentrated to secure the lowest portion of drapery pleats.

Basement Windows - Opposite of awning windows, these windows swing inward due to a hinged bottom.

Basting - A technique used in sewing to temporarily fasten layers of fabric using long loose stitches.

Baton - A rod or wand used to hand draw traverse draperies.

Bay Window - A large projecting type of window made of a group of windows set at angles to each other and joined to each other on some sides.

Bell Valance - A gathered or pleated valance which has a number of bell-like shapes at bottom hemline.

Bias Binding - A strip of fabric used for added strength when binding edges of fabric and closing piping. The fabric is cut in a slanted manner from selvage to selvage.

Bishop's Sleeve Curtains - Tie-back curtains which have been bloused at least two times.

Blind - A hard treatment for a window, consisting of a series of horizontal panels.

Bottom Hem - The turned part forming a finished edge at bottom of drapery.

Bow Window - A large projecting type of window that is curved or semi-circular.

Box Pleat - A fold of cloth sewn into place to create fullness in a drapery. Box pleats are evenly spaced and stitched.

Bracket - Metal piece attached to the wall or casing to support a drapery or curtain rod.

Braid - A ribbon, which is woven, to be used for trimming or added to edges of draperies and accessories.

Bull's-Eye Window - A circular window glazed with flat or arched glass.

Butterfly Pleat - A two-part pleat which flares out at the top and is bar-tacked at the bottom.

C

Café - A traversing or non-traversing drapery, designed as a tier. The heading can be various styles. They can be set at a variety of heights to control ventilation, view and light.

Café Rod - A small, round decorative rod which comes in white, brass or woodgrain finish, used to mount café curtains that do not have a rod pocket. Café rods are meant to be seen and add an additional decorative touch to the curtain treatment.

Canopy - A fabric window topper created by sewing pockets into fabric panels and inserting a rod with a small projection at the top of the panel, a rod with a larger projection at the bottom.

Cantonniere - A three-sided shaped or straight cornice that "frames" the window - across the top and down the two sides. It is made of a hardboard, padded and covered with fabric.

Cape Cod Curtain - A café curtain decorated by a ruffle around the bottom and sides. This is also called a ruffle-round curtain.

Carriers - Small runners installed in a traverse rod which hold a drapery pin or hook.

Cartridge Pleat - A fold of cloth sewn into place to create fullness in a drapery. This is a round pleat 2-2 1/2 inches in depth. Roundness is created by stuffing of crinoline or paper (removed for cleaning).

Cascade - A fall of fabric that descends in a zigzag line from a drapery heading or top treatment.

Cased Heading - A curtain heading with a simple, hemmed top, in which a rod is inserted.

Casement - (1) A cloth drapery that is of an open-weave material but more opaque than a sheer. (2) A type of vertically hinged window, whose panes open by sliding sideways or cranking outward.

Casing (Window) - Wooden frame around a window.

Catchstitch - A stitch used for hemming raw edges, and then covered by a piece of fabric.

Cathedral Window - A window which points upward, and is formed at an angle.

Center Draw - One pair of draperies which draws open and closes exactly at a window's center point.

Center Support - A metal grip which is used to support a traverse rod from above and prevents rod form sagging in the middle, but does not interfere with rod operation.

Clerestory Windows - A series of small windows which let in light and air. These are placed high on the wall to allow complete privacy.

Colonial - A design period common prior to the revolutionary war in America. It is typically dated from 1608 to 1790.

Corbel Bay - A second story bay window.

Cord - A cable yarn which can be made from either cotton or synthetic materials. It is used for various reasons including holding blinds and shades together, and as a means for drawing traverse draperies, shades, and blinds.

Corner Window - A corner window literally wraps a corner of the building at right angles.

Cornice - A shallow, box-like structure, usually made of wood, fastened across the top of a window to conceal the drapery hardware.

Cornice Board - A horizontal board used as support for a cornice or as foundation for swags and tails.

Cornice Pole - A curtain pole having rings, and used for heavy curtains.

Corona Drape - A drapery which is hung at the top of a bed from a semi-circular bracket or a pole.

Cottage Curtains - A term used to describe curtains displayed in a casual or informal manner.

Country Curtains - A casual curtain treatment with ruffles at valance, bottom, sides, and ties. The curtain is shirred at a maximum of five times in fullness, and is usually made with plain or tiny printed fabric.

Coverage - A term used to describe the amount of fullness in fabric at the window.

Crown Glass - A particular type of glass consisting of hand-blown crowns, measuring about one meter in diameter.

Curtain - A window covering either hung from rings, or made with a casing so that it slips over a rod. Curtains are informal window coverings.

Custom Glazing - Unusual sized or oddly shaped window glass, which is custom made and installed.

Custom-Made Draperies - Draperies made to order in a workroom or decorator shop.

Cut Length - The length after allowances have been made for heading and hem.

Cut Width - The width that the fabric should be cut after allowances have been made.

D

Decorator Rods - Hardware used for the purpose of decorating, and meant to be seen in the open. Usually made from chrome, wood, brass, or antique wrought iron.

Diaphanous Sheers - Drapery used for the purpose of daytime privacy. The finely woven transparent fabrics filter out glare. Also know as glass curtains.

Dormer Window - An upright window which breaks the surface of a sloping roof.

Double Hung - May be several items: Double hung window, Double hung shutters, and Double hung draperies (two sets of draperies usually sheer fabric under opaque fabric, both operating independently).

Drapability - How well a fabric can flow or fall into folds in an attractive manner.

Drapery - A window covering which is usually hung from a traverse rod. Draperies most often have pleated headings which may be lined or unlined.

Draw Draperies - Panels of fabric, featuring pleated headings.

Dress Curtains - Curtains used for the sole purpose of decorating. They are not meant to be drawn.

E

Ease - Refers to extra fabric allowance given in order to make the finished length more accurate. Sometimes fabric that was not calculated into the final length will be lost when stitching double fold hems, headings, rod pockets, or when gathering a treatment onto a rod. It is a good idea to add 1/2" ease to the length before cutting to ensure a more accurate finish.

Elements of Design - The elements which make up a design, including: texture, light, color, space, form, shape, pattern, and ornament.

Empire - A design period dating from 1804 to 1820 in France and 1820 to 1860 in America.

End Bracket - The two supporting metal grips which hold a drapery rod to the wall or ceiling. They control the amount of projection.

End Housing - Refers to the box parts at the extreme ends of a traverse drapery rod. They enclose the mechanism through which the cords run.

End Pleat - The final pleat in a drapery, hooked into the end bracket.

English Sash Window - A sliding frame consisting of a number of rectangular shaped glass panels. Also called Renaissance sash.

F

Fabric Finishes - Treatments used to give the fabric more durability, decoration, and usefulness. These can be chemical or mechanical.

Fabric Sliding Panels - Panels of fabric which are drawn with a baton. These are flat, overlapping, and are installed on a track rod.

Face Fabric - The primary fabric on draperies or curtains. This is the fabric which faces the interior of the room.

Facing - A strip of fabric over the main fabric, with the purpose of hiding raw edges and unlined curtains or draperies.

Factory-Made Treatments - Custom specifications in hard window treatments ordered from a manufacturer or factory. These include: shades, shutters, blinds and screens.

Fan Folding - Fan folding helps to obliterate wrinkling, set the folds and give better drapability. This is done by folding pleated draperies into a thin band.

Fascia - A board of rectangular shape, set horizontally with the purpose of covering a curtain heading or shade fixture.

Federal Period - A design period dating from 1790 to 1820. Also called Neoclassic.

Fenestration - Location and proportion of windows in relationship to solid wall areas.

Festoon - A decorative drapery treatment of folded fabric that hangs in a graceful curve, and frames the top of a window. Also called Parisian shade.

Finial - Decorative end piece on café rods or decorative traverse rods (also referred to as "pole ends").

Finished Length - This is the length after draperies have been made, using the extra allowances in hem and heading.

Finished Width - This is the width after draperies have been made. This is found by measuring the length of the mounting board or rod, and then adding in the depth of any returns.

Fixed Glass - Term used to describe windows which are not made to open or close.

Flat Curtain Rod - A curtain rod, different from a traverse rod, because it does not use a pulley and cord to operate.

Flemish Heading - A goblet type of heading where each of the pleats are connected along their base using a hand-sewn cord.

Flounce - A technique adding an extra long heading sewn at top of a rod pocket, and having the curtain fall over the rod pocket, to create the appearance of a short attached valance.

French Door Draw - A swinging door or casement window with one-way traverse rods attached.

French Doors - Doors in a pair, which are lengthwise, mostly made up of glass panes.

French Pleats - This is a three-fold pleat and the one most often used in draperies.

French Seam - A seam most often used when the seam will be visible, or when using lightweight fabrics.

Fringe - An edging with hanging tassels or threads, used as decoration.

Fullness - The proportion of the finished width of the valance or curtain to the length of the mounting board or rod.

G

Gathered Heading - A heading for a curtain or valance, in which the heading is gathered by means of gathering tape.

Gathering Tape - A tape stitched to the top of a curtain to create a gathered effect by pulling on cords which run through the tape.

Gathers - Folding and puckering are formed when pulling on loosely stitched thread.

Georgian Period - A design period which dates from 1700 to 1790.

Glue-Baste - A technique using glue to secure two pieces of fabric together before sewing.

Goblet Heading - A curtain heading having a series of hand-sewn tubes, in which each of their tops are stuffed with padding or contrast fabric.

Goblet Pleats - Similar to pinch pleats, except having the top edge padded and pushed out in a goblet type of shape.

Greenhouse Window - A window that generally extends at a 90-degree angle from the wall, has glass top and sides and two accompanying shelves for plants.

Group Pleat - A set of, generally 3, pleats with space between each one.

H

Half-Canopy -A canopy above a bed in a rectangular shape, which extends only partially from the headboard down the bed.

Heading - The hemmed, usually stiffened, portion across the top of a curtain or drapery.

Hem - Refers to finished sides and bottom edges of a drapery.

Holdback - A decorative piece of hardware that holds draperies to each side of the window.

I

Insert Pulley - An auxiliary traverse rod part, over which the cords operate.

Inside Mount - A treatment installed inside of a window frame.

Installation - A process which undergoes the various aspects of placing and setting a window treatment.

Interlining - A fabric, usually of soft material, sewn in between the curtain and the back lining to improve bulk, insulation, and overall drapability.

Inverted Pleat - A pleat formed the opposite way of a traditional box pleat, in which the edges of the pleat meet in the middle right side of the fabric. Also know as the kick pleat.

J

Jabot - A decorative vertical end of an over treatment that usually finishes a horizontal festoon.

Jalousie Window - A window made up from a number of horizontal slants, delivering good ventilation properties.

Jamb - Interior sides of a door or window frame.

K

Keystone Arch - An arch used as part of a wood molding for decoration. It is rounded and Roman in style.

Knife Pleats - Narrow, finely pressed and closely spaced pleats which all go in the same direction.

L

Lambrequin - A cornice that completely frames the window. Sometimes used interchangeably with valance or cantonniere.

Laminated Weights - Weight covered on both sides to avoid rust marks on drapery.

Lanai - A type of window covering made up of a series of hinged, rigid plastic panels, hung from a traverse track.

Lapped Seam - A seam, which is most useful for matching patterns together on the right sides of two separate pieces of fabric.

Lining - A fabric backing for a drapery.

Lintel - Lintels are wood, steel, or reinforced concrete beams placed over both window and door openings to hold up the wall and roof above.

Lit a la Polonnaise - A drape set made to fall from a center point above a bed.

Lock Stitch - A stitch purposely made loose, to give way for a little movement. An excellent stitch when used for holding together fabrics, linings and interlinings.

Louvers - Slats generally made from metal, wood or plastic. These can be horizontal or vertical and are used for blinds and shutters.

M

Master Carrier - Two arms that overlap in center of rod when draperies are closed, allowing draperies to close completely.

Milium - Trade name for a thermal lining.

Miniblinds - Miniblinds have a series of 1-inch horizontal metal or plastic slats, which are held together with a cord. They can be tilted and lifted. Micro-miniblinds are similar except that the slats are only a 1/2 inch.

Miter - A technique in folding the fabric as to keep excess fabric out of sight and to eliminate bulk.

Mitered Corner - The formation of the bottom edge of drapery with a 45-degree angle on hem side.

Modern Period - A design period dating from 1900 to present.

Mullion - The vertical wood or masonry sections between a series of window frames.

Multi-Draw - A simultaneous opening and closing of several draperies on one rod at one time.

Muntin - The horizontal wood strips that separate panes of glass in windows.

N

Neoclassic Period - A design period dating from 1760 to 1789 in France, 1770 to 1820 in England and 1790 to 1820 in America.

Notch - A tiny cut, usually in a v-shape, at the edge of a fabric.

O

Off-Center - A window not centered on a wall. Draperies still meet at its center point.

One-Way Draw - Drapery designed to draw one way only, in one panel.

Opacity - A degree measuring the amount to which solid material blocks view and light.

Open Cuff - This is on the backside of drapery and at top. Open cuffs make one of the strongest type headings on any drapery. This results when you carry both fabrics to the top and make a turn with the crinoline.

Oriel Bay - Similar to a corbel bay window, but having the second story window descend down to the first floor.

Orientation - A term used to describe the direction in which a window faces, north, east, south or west.

Outside Mount - A treatment installed over and to the side of a window frame on the wall.

Overdraperies - A layer of drapery fabric which is installed over an existing layer of drapery.

Overlap - The overlap of a pair of draperies is that part of a drapery panel, which rides the master carrier of a traverse rod, and overlaps in the center when draperies are drawn closed. Usually 3 1/2" on each side.

P

Padded Edge - A fabric border rolled and stuffed to form a long round shape.

Palladian Window - A window consisting of a high, rounded, middle section and two lower squared sections at each side. Also know as a Venetian Window.

Panel - One half of a pair of draperies or curtains.

Passementerie - This term is used to describe the vast range of trimmings and decorative edges.

Pattern Repeat - The distance between any given point in a design to where that exact point is repeated again.

Pelmet - A upholstered wood cornice or stiffened and shaped valance.

Pencil Pleat Heading - A heading for a curtain which is formed by a certain tape, where as when drawn up it creates a column of tightly packed folds.

Period Window Treatment - Refers to historically designed treatments from any specific design period.

Picture Window - A type of window with a large center glass area with usually two smaller glass areas on each side.

Pinch Pleats - A drapery heading where the basic pleat is divided into two or three smaller, equal pleats, sewn together at the bottom edge on the right side of the fabric.

Pin-On-Hook - A metal pin to fasten draperies to a rod. It pins into drapery pleat and hooks to traverse carrier or café rod.

Piping - Cords used at the edges of a curtain for added effects, usually fabric covered and put in through a seam.

Pivot - While sewing corners, this technique has one stop the machine with the needle down in the fabric still, and then turn the fabric at the corner before continuing to stitch.

Plate Glass - A design which was popular from the seventeenth century to the nineteenth century in France. Molten glass is ironed smooth after being poured onto a table, and then made into large sheets.

Pleat - A fold of cloth sewn into place to create fullness.

Pleat To - The finished width of the fabric after it has been pleated. Example: A width of 48" fabric has been pleated to 18" - "Pleat To" 18".

Pleater Tape - Pocketed heading material designed to be used with pleating hooks.

Polonnaise - A bed set against the wall lengthwise, having a small ascending dome.

Portiere - A term used to describe a doorway treatment, either a hung curtain or drapery.

Pouf Shade - Shades or valances with a soft looking fabric and a gathered hem.

Pressing - An important part of sewing technique. With an iron selected to the appropriate setting for a particular fabric, a steaming method is used by lifting the iron up and pressing it down, instead of sliding it across the fabric in a traditional ironing way.

Principles of Design - The theory of design made possible by manipulating the elements of design to create proper balance, emphasis, proportion and scale.

Priscilla Curtains - Curtains with ruffled valance, sides, bottom, hem and ties. They are usually made from sheer or opaque fabrics and sometimes they meet in the center or cross in center.

Projection - Refers to a jutting out, an extension. On a curtain or drapery rod, it is that part which returns to the wall from the front of the rod.

Protractor - A drapery tool by which exact angles are measured (as in bay windows).

R

Railroading - Some decorator fabrics use railroading in correspondence to widths for floor-length treatments. In this technique the lengthwise grain runs in a horizontal manner across the window treatment, making vertical seams unnecessary.

Ready-Mades - Standard size draperies, factory-made and available at local stores or through mail order sources.

Renaissance Period - A design period dating from 1400 to 1600 in Italy, 1589 to 1643 in France and 1558 to 1649 in England. An era full of art, literature, architecture and science.

Repeat - The space from one design motif to the next one on a patterned fabric.

Return - The distance from the face of the rod to the wall of casing where the bracket is attached.

Reveals - Sides to a window opening, with right angles facing the wall and window.

Rococo Period - A French design period dating from 1730 to 1760, where decorations were curved, asymmetrical and ornamental.

Rod - A metal or plastic device from which curtains are hung. It is used when a pole is not being used. Double rods are used for two layers of fabric.

Rod Pocket - A hollow sleeve in the top - and sometimes the bottom - of a curtain or drapery through which a rod is inserted. The rod is then attached to a solid wall surface.

Rod Width - Measures the width between the end of a bracket to the end of the other bracket including the stack-back and window width.

Roller Shade - A shade operated by a device with a spring. When the spring is let loose, the shade coils itself around the device's cylinder.

Roman Shade - A corded shade with rods set horizontally in back to give the shade a number of neat side-set pleats or folds when raised.

RTB - Rod top and bottom.

Ruching - A thin area of pleated or gathered fabric, often used for trimming or tie-backs.

Ruffle - A decorative trimming consisting of a strip of gathered fabric.

R-Value - A window treatment, ceiling or wall's capacity to keep heat in or out.

S

Sash - A wooden frame used to hold the glass of swinging and sliding windows, around either a door or window.

Sash Curtain - Any sheer material hung close to the window glass. Usually hung from spring tension rods or sash rods mounted inside the window casing.

Sash Rod - A small rod, either decorative or plain, usually mounted inside a window frame on the sash.

Scalloped Heading - A popular top treatment for café curtains featuring semi-circular spaces between curtain rings.

Seam - The stitching of two pieces of fabric together at right sides, leaving the stitches hidden behind on the wrong side of the fabric, for a clean finished look on the right side.

Seam Allowance - A slim extra allowance in the fabric between the line for stitching and the raw edge of the fabric.

Selvedge - The tightly woven edge on a width of fabric to hold the fabric together.

Shade - A window covering usually made from cloth or vinyl that covers the glass, and rolls up or down off of the window.

Sheet Glass - Popular in the twenty first century, large sheets of glass are created by casting or drawing and then used for glazing.

Shirring - A rod that is smaller than the fabric width is slid through a rod pocket to create a gathered effect in the fabric.

Shoji Screen - An oriental design using a wood grid to attach paper, forming a translucent effect in sliding or stationary panels.

Shutters - A series of folding wood panels, which are hung by a side hinge.

Side Hem - The turned part forming a finished edge at the side of the drapery.

Sill - The horizontal "ledge-like" portion of a window casing.

Skylights - A window set into a ceiling or roof, made from glass or plastic.

Slides - Small runners installed in a traverse rod which hold a drapery pin or hook.

Slip Stitch - Matching colored thread is used to stitch the folded edge of a lining to the base fabric.

Smocked Heading - A curtain heading consisting of a honeycomb effect. A heading full of pencil pleats hooked together at specific spacing give this effect.

Spacing - Refers to the flat space between pleats; the fuller the drapery, the less the spacing.

Spanish Arch - A rounded arch designed in a Spanish fashion.

Stacking - The area required for draperies when they are completely opened. Also referred to as stackback.

Swag - A section of draped fabric above a window.

T

Tails - Shaped and stiffened, or free falling, hanging trails of fabric from the end of swags.

Tambour Curtains - Curtains that originally were used as folk craft in Scandinavia, they are lightweight or sheer fabrics, embroidered.

Tape-Gathered Heading - A gathered effect for curtain headings, using thin threaded tape sewn onto the top of a curtain and then pulled by the parallel threads.

Tension Pulley - The pulley attachment through which the traverse cords move for one continuous smooth operation when drapery is drawn. May be mounted on a baseboard, casing or wall, on one or both sides.

Tester - A canopy supported by a bed with tall corner posts.

Tie - A thin strip of fabric which is used with tie-backs to secure a drapery to a wall. The tie can be decorated or shaped.

Tie-backs - Decorative pieces of hardware, sometimes called holdbacks. Available in many forms and designed to hold draperies back from the window to allow light passage or add an additional decorative touch to the window treatment.

Tier - Curtain layers arranged one above the other with a normal overlap of 4". Upper tiers project from the wall at a greater distance than lower panels to allow each curtain to hang free.

Traverse - To draw across. A traverse drapery is one that opens or closes across a window by means of the traverse rod from which it is hung.

Traverse Rod - A rod which is operated by a cord and pulley.

Turkish Bed - A thin bed set back into a draped alcove.

U

Under-Draperies - A lightweight drapery, usually a sheer, closest to the window glass. It hangs beneath a heavier over-drapery.

V

Valance - A valance is a horizontal decorative fabric treatment used at the top of draperies to screen hardware and cords.

Victorian - A design period dating from 1837 to 1910 in England and 1840 to 1920 in America.

W

Wall Fasteners - Window treatments are fastened to hollow walls using toggle bolts or molly bolts.

Weave - The act of interlacing when forming a piece of fabric.

Weights - (chain and lead) Lead weights are sewn in at the vertical seams and each corner of drapery panel. Chain weights are small beads strung in a line along bottom hemline of sheers, to insure an even hemline and straight hanging.

Width - A word to describe a single width of fabric. Several widths of fabric are sewn together to make a panel of drapery. "Panel" is sometimes used in referring to a width of fabric.

Z

Zigzag Stitch - One of various sewing machine settings. In this stitch the needle moves back and forth, at the desired length and width, in a zigzag pattern. This stitch is often used for finishing seams.

Glossary of Fabric Terms

A

Acetate - Used to make many persuasive artificial silks. It has similar draping and finish qualities as silk but less likely to rot or fade.

Acrylic - A soft lightweight fabric made from a synthetic long-chain polymer, primarily made up of acrylonitrile.

Aluminum-Coated - A lining used to help exclude light, heat and cold. It is not visible, as it faces inside the fabric, while the outside of the fabric shows woven cream cotton.

Antique Satin - One of the most common drapery fabrics sold. Characterized by a lustrous effect, normally composed of rayon/ acetate blends.

B

Baize - Similar to flannel, dyed green or red. Mostly used for lining in silverware drawers and card tables. It's texture and color make it convenient for improvised shades or curtains. Fades in sunlight.

Basketweave - Plain under-and-over weave; primarily in draperies.

Batik - A dyeing technique developed in Java, where dye is applied and then washed, leaving bold patterns.

Batiste - A soft finished fabric, which has a high count of fine yarns. It is more opaque than voiles. Usually composed of 100% polyester or a polyester blend.

Batting - A man-made fluffy fiber, used for padding edges.

Bias - A diagonal line which intersects the crosswise and lengthwise grain of any fabric. Woven fabrics, which do not stretch at the crosswise or lengthwise grains, do stretch at the bias.

Blackout - A heavy interlining where a layer of opaque material is placed between two pieces of cotton to block out any light. Improves the drapability qualities. It is most often white or cream.

Boucle - French for curled, indicates a curled or looped surface.

Broadcloth - (1) A medium to heavyweight twill blend or worsted wool fabric which is napped and felted. (2) A cotton fabric similar to muslin, due to its fine crosswise cords.

Brocade - Rich jacquard - woven fabric with all-over interwoven design of raised figures or flowers. Brocade has a raised surface in contrast to felt damask, and is generally made of silk, rayon and nylon yarns with or without metallic treatment.

Brocatelle - Usually made of silk or wool, with brocade similarities.

Bump - Interlining imported from England, heavy weight, cotton, and available bleached or unbleached. Similar to table felt and reinforcement felt, but slightly stiffer. Cotton flannel is often used instead of bump.

Burlap - Coarse, canvas-like fabric made of jute, hemp or cotton. Also called Gunny.

C

Canvas - A heavy woven cotton and linen blend. Similar to cotton duck.

Casements - Open weave casual fabric, characterized by its instability.

Challis - One of the softest fabrics made. Normally made of rayon and also combined with cotton.

Cheesecloth - Cheap and loosely woven, this fabric will easily fade, wrinkle and shrink. Similar to muslin.

Chiffon - A transparent sheer fabric, given a soft finish.

Chintz - Glazed cotton fabric often printed with gay figures and large flower designs. Some glazes will wash out in laundering. The only durable glaze is a resin finish which will withstand washing or dry cleaning. Unglazed chintz is called cretonne.

Corduroy - A cut filling-pile cloth with narrow to wide wales which run in the warp direction of the goods and made possible by the use of an extra set of filling yarns in the construction. The back is of plain or twill weave, the latter affording the better construction. Washable types are available and stretch and durable press garments of corduroy are very popular. Usually an all-cotton cloth, some of the goods are now made with nylon or rayon pile effect on a cotton backing fabric or with polyester-cotton blends.

Cotton - An inexpensive versatile fiber which can be printed, dyed and finished in numerous ways. It also has the ability to be made colorfast and withstand light and heat. It is popular among furnishing fabrics when used alone or as a cotton blend. Its shortcomings include crushing and mildewing.

Cotton Duck - A cotton differing in weight from 7 to 15 oz. per yard. Heavier types are ideal for no-sew curtains due to the fact that lining is unnecessary and the edges can be glued or pinked.

Cotton Lawn - Finely woven cotton, given an extremely smooth finish.

Crash - A coarse fabric having a rough irregular surface obtained by weaving thick uneven yarns. Usually cotton or linen, sometimes spun rayon or blends.

Cretonne - A cotton fabric usually having printed floral or angular shapes. It is a plain weave, unglazed and coarser than chintz.

Crewelwork - Indian Cotton, wool or linen fabric adorned with wool chain stitching. Most often on a cream background. Used as early American and English bed hangings.

Crinoline - A heavily sized, stiff fabric used as a foundation to support the edge of a hem or puffed sleeve. Also used as interlining. This is also referred to as Buckram.

Crosswise Grain - Crosswise grain runs perpendicular to the selvages on woven fabric.

D

Dacron - A synthetic fiber with good filling and padding qualities.

Damask - Firm, glossy jacquard-patterned fabric. Damask is Similar to brocade, but flatter and reversible. It can be made from linen, cotton, rayon or silk, or a combination of fibers.

Denim - A sturdy fabric, mostly in dark blue, twill weave. Also called jean.

Domette - A lightweight cotton interlining imported from England. Similar to American needle-punched fleece. It is used with light shades, curtains and swags.

Dotted Swiss - A sheer fabric with opaque dots,

sometimes given a raised texture.

Double Knit - A fabric knitted with a double stitch on a double needle frame to provide a double thickness and is the same on both sides. It has excellent body and stability.

Dupion - Textured, real or synthetic silk. It is light-weight, which gives this fabric the tendency to rot or fade. Synthetic dupion is made from viscose and acetate. The real silk dupion is usually imported from India.

E

Eyelet - Embroidered white cotton fabric often used for shades left unlined, or light curtains.

F

Fabric Identification Label - This label will tell the fiber content, width, and care method for the fabric, and sometimes the pattern repeat. The fabric identification label is found on the bolt or tube of fabric.

Faille - Plain weave (flat-rib); with filling yarns heavier than warp.

Figured Material - A fabric whose pattern is created from the structure of the weave.

Foamback - Term used to denote that a fabric has been laminated to a backing of polyurethane foam.

Fusible Buckram - A strip of white cotton filled with glue and used as a stiffener. Good for use inside of hand-pleated headings to avoid the visibility of machine stitching. It is fused to the fabric with a hot iron.

Fusible Heavyweight Buckram - An open-weave stiffener, made from jute and filled with glue. It is used for the base of a cornice. A hot iron will fuse it in place, releasing the glue.

G

Gauze - A sheer, but coarse fabric, available in a variety of thread thicknesses.

Gimp - A wind of fabric which can be stiffened with wire or cord.

Gingham - A cheap classic cotton fabric with a checkered pattern. The checkers come in a variety of sizes and mostly primary colors.

Glassing - Thin finish provides luster, sheen, shine or polish to some fabrics. Chintz is an example of a glazed fabric.

Grosgrain - A silk fabric with a ribbed texture on surface.

H

Hand, Handle - The reaction of the sense of touch, when fabrics are held in the hand. There are many factors which give "character or individuality" to a material observed through handling. A correct judgment may thus be made concerning its capabilities in content, working properties, drapability, feel, elasticity, fineness and softness, launderability, etc.

Herringbone - A versatile medium weight fabric with a zigzag pattern, named after the spine of the herring fish. It is a novelty twill weave, available mostly in neutral colors. Also called Chevron.

Holland - A linen or cotton medium-weight fabric, fade resistant and sturdy, also stiffened with oil or shellac. It is standard for valances and roller shades due to its non-fraying edges.

I

Ikat - Chinese cotton or silk fabric with faint geometric patterns due to a process of tie dying.

Inherent Flame Frees - Fabric woven of flame-resistant fabric (not processed) and flame-free for life of the fabric.

Interfacing - A fabric stiffener used to give support and hold the shape of the fabric.

J

Jacquard - A loom which can produce woven patterns in a variety of colors. The patterns are known for being intricate and large.

Jute - An inexpensive, easily available and long lasting fabric. It can be dyed and comes in a neutral color. Like linen, it is one of the most important fabrics.

K

Khaki - A beige or earth toned, plain or twill weave fabric with a wide range of uses.

L

Lace - Openwork fabric generally made from cotton, created from twisting and knotting threads against a net-like background to form the desired design. Lace has an endless variety of designs. It is convenient for glass curtains.

Lengthwise Grain - Fabrics are typically stronger along the lengthwise grain. The lengthwise grain runs parallel to the selvages on woven fabric.

Linen - This is a product of the flax plant. Among the properties of linen are rapid moisture absorption, no fuzziness, does not soil quickly, a neutral luster and stiffness.

Linen Union - Cotton linen blend fabric, durable and reasonably priced.

M

Madras Cotton - Inexpensive Indian cotton, woven in a checkered, plaid or striped fashion, brightly colored. Sometimes referred to as sari fabric.

Marquisette - Usually made from synthetic fibers, an open mesh and thin fabric.

Matelasse - Appearance of a quilted weave; figured pattern with a raised, bubbly surface.

Mesh - A term used to describe textiles or open-weave fabrics having a net-like structure.

Modacrylic - A modified fiber in which the fiber-forming substance of any long-chain synthetic polymer is composed of less than 85%, but at least 25% of weight of acrylonitrile units.

Mohair - Comes from the Angora goat. It is lighter weight drapery fabric; slightly brushed or hairy finish.

Moiré - A finish given cotton, silk, acetate, rayon, nylon, etc., where bright and dim effects are observed. This is achieved by passing the fabric between engraved rollers which press the particular motif into the fabric.

Moreen - A heavyweight fabric in a wool or wool and cotton blend fabric, usually having a watered pattern.

Muslin - Usually in white or off-white color, this fabric is sheer and delicately woven, but strong.

N

Ninon - A smooth, transparent, high textured type of voile fabric. Usually made from 100% polyester.

Non-Fusible Buckram - A medium-weight cotton stiffener, used to sew into tie-backs.

Non-Fusible Heavyweight Buckram - Two-ply double starched stiffener made from jute; unlike fusible heavyweight buckram, it is sewn onto the cornice instead of fused. It is also easier to clean than the fusible kind.

Nylon - A durable and versatile fabric, made up from a long-chain polymer, originating from petroleum, air, natural gas and water. It has remarkable strength and is moderately priced.

O

Olefin - A wax-like fiber, made from petroleum products. It is lightweight but strong, and inexpensive.

Ombre - A graduate or shade effect of color used in a striped motif. Usually ranges from light to dark tones. Also called jaspe or strie.

Organdy - Very light and thin, transparent, stiff and wiry cotton cloth. Will withstand repeated launderings and still retain its crispness. Organdy is a true, durable finish cloth.

P

Padding - A soft and bulky fabric used for stuffing or filling.

Paisley - A timeless motif, this fine woolen cloth has detailed pine, floral or scroll type designs printed or woven onto it.

Plaid - A fabric which can be printed or woven with rectangular and square shapes in a variety of colors.

Plush - A favorite of the Victorian era, this fabric is an old fashioned form of velvet made from wool, mohair, and less often cotton, with a deeper but more thinly scattered pile. Now in modern times it is man made.

Polyester - A stable fabric which displays excellent drapability. This fabric can be woven or knit.

Poplin - Sometimes printed decoratively, this is a plain weave with raised, circular weft cords created with large filling threads. Can be cotton, blend or synthetic and has a variety of uses.

R

Raw Edge - The edge of a fabric which is cut, having neither selvage nor hem.

Rayon - Displays a texture similar to silk, in touch and visibility. Rayon is available in a vast range of textures and types.

Repp - A fabric having ribbed qualities or appearance.

S

Saran - A plastic vinyl fiber, durable and colorfast.

Sateen - A firmly woven, strong cotton or cotton blend fabric, usually having stripes or bright solid colors. The finish is smooth and shiny.

Satin Weave - One of the three basic weaves, the others being plain weave and the twill weave. The surface of satin weave cloth is almost made up entirely of warp or filling floats since in the repeat of the weave, each yarn of the one system passes or floats over or under all but one yarn of the opposite yarn system. Satin weaves have a host of uses - brocade, brocatelle, damask other decorative materials.

Selvage - Each side edge of a woven fabric and an actual part of the warp in the goods. Other names for it are listing, self-edge, and raw edge.

Shantung - An inconsistently textured raw silk, at one time hand woven in China's Shantung Province.

Silk - The only natural fiber that comes in a filament form, reeled from the cocoon, cultivated or wild.

Slub Yarn - Yarn of any type which is irregular in diameter; may be caused by error, or purposely made with slubs to bring out some desired effect to enhance a material.

Suede Cloth - A fabric made to be similar to suede

leather in visibility and touch.

T

Taffeta - A fine plain weave fabric smooth on both sides, usually with a sheen on its surface.

Tapestry - A heavy well insulating fabric, at one time made in replication of hand-sewn tapestries, but is now produced on a jacquard loom.

Tartan - A woolen cloth fabric made up of a specific checkered pattern, having particular colors of a certain Scottish clan. This fabric has great insulating qualities.

Terry Cloth - This cloth fabric has uncut loops on both sides of the cloth. Terry is also made on a jacquard loom to form interesting motifs.

Texture - (1) The actual number of warp threads and filling picks per inch in any cloth that has been woven. (2) The finish and appearance of cloth.

Thread Count - (1) The actual number of warp ends and filling picks per inch in a woven cloth. Texture is another name for this term. (2) In knitted fabric, thread count implies the number of wales or ribs, and the courses per inch.

Ticking - A striped cotton fabric, traditionally made up of only black and white, but now ticking comes in a wide variety of colors. It is used for covering mattresses, cushion pads, or can be made into curtains and shades.

Tricot - Usually made from nylon, this soft and thin fabric is made with crosswise elastic ribs in the back, and non-elastic on top. It is seldom used for draperies due to its lack of body, but is beneficial for custom sheeting.

Tussah Silk - A raw, typically Indian silk, in a yellowish-brown color, difficult to dye.

V

Velour - (1) A term loosely applied to cut pile cloths in general; also to fabrics with a fine raised finish. (2) A cut pile cotton fabric comparable with cotton velvet, but with a greater and denser pile. (3) A staple, high-grade woolen fabric which has a close, fine, dense, erect, and even nap which provides a soft, pleasing hand.

Velvet - A warp pile cloth in which a succession of rows of short cut pile stand so close together as to give an even, uniform surface. When the pile is more than one-eighth of an inch high, the cloth is usually called Plus.

Viscose (Rayon) - The most ancient of man-made fiber, well know for its distinctive sheen used in highlighting patterns, and ability to add luster and strength to cotton and silk blends.

Voile - A thin open mesh cloth made by a variation of plain weave. Most voiles are made of polyester. Similar to ninon, but with a much finer denier of yarn with a very soft, drapable hand.

W

Warp - The yarns which run vertically or lengthwise in woven fabric.

Weft Yarn - The yarn runs horizontal or cross yarns.

Wool - An expensive versatile fabric which comes from the fleece of domesticated sheep. It has excellent insulating uses and is wrinkle and flame resistant.

Worsted - Fabric made of twisted yarn, of a wool type.

Textile Fibers and Their Properties

NATURAL FIBERS

COTTON

Drapability: excellent hang, soft hand
Color fastness: good, vat dyes best
Sun resistance: excellent, does not sun rot
Abrasion resistance: excellent
Sagging: does not stretch, except when wet
Resiliency: poor, packs easily, wrinkles easily, very absorbent, burns
Care: wash or dry clean and iron at high temperature

Cotton generally wears excellently in drapery (print or plains).

LINEN OR FLAX

Drapability: good hang, but not as soft as cotton
Color fastness: good to poor, prints do not hold their color as well as plain fabrics
Sun resistance: excellent, does not sun rot
Abrasion resistance: excellent
Sagging: strong, does not stretch
Resiliency: poor, packs badly, does wrinkle
Care: dry clean and iron at high temperature

Linens are excellent in plain and casement fabric and good in prints.

SILK

Drapability: good hang, medium to soft hand
Color fastness: good
Sun resistance: poor, rots in short time, lining helps
Abrasion resistance: good
Sagging: strong, does not sag
Resiliency: good, does not pack badly
Care: dry clean and iron at medium temperature

Little silk is used in drapery today. This is due to sun rot and cost.

WOOL

There is virtually none used in drapery fabric.

MAN-MADE

RAYON

Drapability: good hang, soft hand
Color fastness: good to excellent (solution dyed)
Sun resistance: good, but not as good as cotton or linen
Abrasion resistance: good, but not as good as nylon or cotton
Sagging: poor, stretches in loose yarns, but OK in tight woven fabrics
Resiliency: good, does not pack, wrinkles less than cotton or linen
Care: dry clean and iron at medium temperature

Rayon is blended with other fibers: cotton, acetate and linen.

ACETATE

Drapability: good hand, soft hand
Color fastness: good (solution dyed)
Sun resistance: good, not as good as cotton and linen
Abrasion resistance: good, but not as good as cotton or nylon
Sagging: poor stretches in loose yarns, but OK in tight woven fabrics
Resiliency: good, does not pack, wrinkles less than cotton or linen
Care: dry clean and iron at low temperature

Blends well with other fibers, rayon and nylon.

POLYESTER

Drapability: excellent hang, very soft hand
Color fastness: good to excellent
Sun resistance: excellent
Abrasion resistance: good, sheers must be handled with care. Fabric can be bruised.
Sagging: excellent, does not stretch or shrink
Resiliency: good to excellent, does not pack, wrinkle free
Care: wash or dry clean and iron at low temperature temperature

Polyester is an excellent fabric for most drapery applications. It blends well with other fibers. In polyester cotton blends, cotton wrinkles less.

NYLON

Drapability: good, soft to stiff hand, not as soft as polyesters
Color fastness: good to excellent
Sun resistance: poor
Abrasion resistance: excellent
Sagging: excellent, does not sag
Resiliency: excellent, does not pack, wrinkle free
Care: dry clean and iron at low temperature

Nylon is not widely used in drapery fabric.

ACRYLIC

Drapability: excellent, very soft hand
Color fastness: excellent, if solution dyed
Sun resistance: excellent, good as cotton or linen
Abrasion resistance: good
Sagging: very good, does not stretch
Resiliency: very good, does not pack and wrinkle free
Care: dry clean and iron at low temperature 50°

Acrylic fabrics hang well and do not sag. Can be blended with polyester. Modacrylics are flameproof.

DYNEL

Drapability: excellent, soft hand like acrylic
Color fastness: excellent
Sun resistance: good to excellent
Abrasion resistance: excellent
Sagging: excellent compared to rayon or acetate
Resiliency: very good, does not pack, wrinkle free, low flamability
Care: Wash only, ironing does not affect it much, use low heat

Drapery Fabrics - Look and Performance

Satins and Jacquards
Usually the most formal and traditional, they are generally made from tightly woven, heavy, soft material which hangs straight from top to bottom in (formal) folds.

Casements, Open Weaves
These have a lighter, more casual feel. They are usually made from loosely woven, textured yarns that hang in looser folds than the formal satins and Jacquards.

Sheers
Made of soft, see-through fabrics, sheers are appropriate in most decors. Light and airy, they are sometimes used in combination with heavier draperies in more formal settings. They are billowy unless weighted, and can be made to drape quite well.

Prints
Suitable in most decors, prints are made from a light, tightly woven fabric, usually cotton or cotton-polyester blends.

Drapery Linings
Linings add substantially to the luxurious appearance necessary for good window treatments, and also provide a fuller pleated look for maintaining a soft drapable hand.

The lined-look provides uniformity to the exterior appearance of a home while allowing a broad choice of textures, weaves, colors and patterns for the interior.

The combination of sunlight and air pollution will eventually take its toll on all colors. There is no such thing as an absolutely colorfast material or dye. Some colors, however will show fading more dramatically than others. Bright colors tend to show fading more than subdued tones, and solids before prints.

Linings help draperies last longer. They afford some protection against sun and fading. They also protect the draperies from water stains — either from condensation on the inside of the window or from a sudden shower.

Insulated linings contribute to energy conservation, keeping homes cooler in summer and warmer in winter.

MEASUREMENT CONVERSION CHART

Inches

Feet	0	1	2	3	4	5	6	7	8	9	10	11
				Metres and millimetres								
0		25	51	76	102	127	152	178	203	229	254	279
1	305	330	356	381	406	432	457	483	508	533	559	584
2	610	635	660	686	711	737	762	787	813	838	864	889
3	914	940	965	991	1.016	1.041	1.067	1.092	1.118	1.143	1.168	1.194
4	1.219	1.245	1.270	1.295	1.321	1.346	1.372	1.397	1.422	1.448	1.473	1.499
5	1.524	1.549	1.575	1.600	1.626	1.651	1.676	1.702	1.727	1.753	1.778	1.803
6	1.829	1.854	1.880	1.905	1.930	1.956	1.981	2.007	2.032	2.057	2.083	2.108
7	2.134	2.159	2.184	2.210	2.235	2.261	2.286	2.311	2.337	2.362	2.388	2.413
8	2.438	2.464	2.489	2.515	2.540	2.565	2.591	2.616	2.642	2.667	2.692	2.718
9	2.743	2.769	2.794	2.819	2.845	2.870	2.896	2.921	2.946	2.972	2.997	3.023
10	3.048	3.073	3.098	3.124	3.150	3.175	3.200	3.226	3.251	3.277	3.302	3.327
11	3.353	3.378	3.404	3.429	3.454	3.480	3.505	3.531	3.556	3.581	3.607	3.632
12	3.658	3.683	3.708	3.734	3.759	3.785	3.810	3.835	3.861	3.886	3.912	3.937
13	3.962	3.988	4.013	4.039	4.064	4.089	4.115	4.140	4.166	4.191	4.216	4.242
14	4.267	4.293	4.318	4.343	4.369	4.394	4.420	4.445	4.470	4.496	4.521	4.547
15	4.572	4.597	4.623	4.648	4.674	4.699	4.724	4.750	4.775	4.801	4.826	4.851
16	4.877	4.902	4.928	4.953	4.978	5.004	5.029	5.055	5.080	5.105	5.131	5.156
17	5.182	5.207	5.232	5.258	5.283	5.309	5.334	5.359	5.385	5.410	5.436	5.461
18	5.486	5.512	5.537	5.563	5.588	5.613	5.639	5.664	5.690	5.715	5.740	5.766
19	5.791	5.817	5.842	5.867	5.893	5.918	5.944	5.969	5.994	6.020	6.045	6.071
20	6.096	6.121	6.147	6.172	6.198	6.223	6.248	6.274	6.299	6.325	6.350	6.375
21	6.401	6.426	6.452	6.477	6.502	6.528	6.553	6.579	6.604	6.629	6.655	6.680
22	6.706	6.731	6.756	6.782	6.807	6.833	6.858	6.883	6.909	6.934	6.960	6.985
23	7.010	7.036	7.061	7.087	7.112	7.137	7.163	7.188	7.214	7.239	7.264	7.290
24	7.315	7.341	7.366	7.391	7.417	7.442	7.468	7.493	7.518	7.544	7.569	7.595
25	7.620	7.645	7.671	7.696	7.722	7.747	7.772	7.798	7.823	7.849	7.874	7.899
26	7.925	7.950	7.976	8.001	8.026	8.052	8.077	8.103	8.128	8.153	8.179	8.204
27	8.230	8.255	8.280	8.306	8.331	8.357	8.382	8.407	8.433	8.458	8.484	8.509
28	8.534	8.560	8.585	8.611	8.636	8.661	8.687	8.712	8.738	8.763	8.788	8.814
29	8.839	8.865	8.890	8.915	8.941	8.966	8.992	9.017	9.042	9.068	9.093	9.119
30	9.144											

Bibliography

Arched Window Solutions
Diane Deeds
1stBooks Library, 2000

Authentic Decor: The
Domestic Interior 1620-1920
Peter Thornton
Seven Dials, 2001

Beautiful Windows: Stylish
Solutions from Hunter Douglas
Window Fashions
Meredith Books, 2001

Caroline Wrey's Complete
Curtain Making Course
Overlook Press, 1997

Complete Book of Window
Treatments & Curtains:
Traditional & Innovative Ways
to Dress Up Your Windows
Carol Parks
Lark Books, 1995

Creative Curtainmaking Made
Easy
Heather Luke
Watson-Guptill, 2001

Creative Window Treatments
(Creating Your Home)
Betterway, 1996

The Curtain Book: A
Sourcebook for Distinctive
Curtains, Drapes, and Shades
for Your Home
Caroline Clifton-Mogg, et al
Bulfinch Press, 1995

The Curtain Sketchbook 2
Wendy Baker
Randall International, 1999

Curtains
Creative Publishing
International, 1998

Curtains: A Design Source
Book
Caroline Clifton-Mogg
Ryland Peters & Small, 2001

Curtains and Draperies:
History, Design, Inspiration
Jenny Gibbs
Overlook Press, 1994

Curtains, Blinds & Valances
(Sew in a Weekend Series)
Editors at Eaglemoss
Betterway, 1998

Curtains, Draperies & Shades
The Editors of Southern Living
Sunset Publishing Company,
2000

Curtains for Beginners (Seams
Sew Easy)
Creative Publishing
International, 1998

Design and Make Curtains
and Drapes
Heather Luke
Storey Books, 1996

Encyclopedia of Curtains:
Complete Curtain Maker
Catherine Merrick, et al
Randall International, 1996

Fabrications: Over 1000 Ways
to Decorate Your Home with
Fabric
Katrin Cargill, et al
Little, Brown & Company,
1999

Great Window Treatments
Claire Martens
Sterling Publications, 1998

House Beautiful Windows
Sally Clark, et al
Hearst Books, 1997

How to Dress a Naked
Window
Donna Babylon
Krause Publications, 1997

Ideas for Great Window
Treatments
Christine Barnes, et al
Sunset Publishing Company,
2000

Interiors: An Introduction
Karla J. Nielson, David A.
Taylor
McGraw-Hill Higher Education,
1994

Judith Miller's Guide to Period-
Style Curtains and Soft
Furnishings
The Overlook Press, 2000

Low Sew Window Treatments
(Creative Textiles)
Creative Publishing
International, 1997

Make It With Style: Window
Shades
Donna Lang, et al
Clarkson Potter, 1997

Make Your Own Curtains &
Blinds
Lani Van Reenen, et al
Storey Books, 1994

Making Curtains & Blinds
Dorothy Wood
Southwater, 2001

More Creative Window
Treatments: Complete step-
by-step instructions with full-
color photos for over 60 distinctive window treatments
Creative Publishing
International, 2000

The New Draperies in the Low
Countries and England
Negley B. Harte
Oxford University Press, 1998

Sew a Beautiful Window:
Innovative Window Treatments
for Every Room in the House
Sally Cowan
Krause Publications, 2001

Sheer Style
Tessa Evelegh
Laurel Glen, 2000

Simply Window Treatments
Sunset Publishing Company,
1999

The Smart Approach to
Window Decor
Lynn Elliott, et al
Creative Homeowner Press,
2000

Southern Living Curtains,
Draperies & Shades
Sunset Publishing Company,
2000

Textile Fabrics and Their
Selection
Isabel Wingate
Prentice Hal, 1970

Two-Hour Window Treatments
Linda Durbano, et al
Sterling Publications, 2001

Practical Home Decorating:
Curtain and Shades
Melanie Paine
Reader's Digest Adult, 1997

A Portfolio of Window &
Window Treatment Ideas
Creative Publishing
International, 1995

The Ultimate Curtain Book: A
Comprehensive Guide to
Creating Your Window
Treatments
Isabella Forbes
Readers Digest, 2000

Victorian and Edwardian
Décor
Jeremy Cooper
Abbeville Press, 1987

Victorian Interior Decoration
Roger W. Moss, Gail C.
Winkler
Henry Holt, 1992

Victorian Style
Judith Miller and Martin Miller
Mitchell Beazley, 1993

What's in Style: Window
Treatments
Megan Connelly
Creative Homeowner Press,
2001

Window Decor
Susan E. Mickey
Sterling Publications, 2001

Window Dressing: From the
Editors of Vogue & Butterick
Butterick Company Inc, 2000

Window Style: Blinds Curtains
Screens Shutters
Mary Fox Linton
Bulfinch Press, 2000

Window Treatments
Linda Hallam
Better Homes & Gardens
Books, 1997

Window Treatments (Singer
Sewing Reference Library)
Creative Publishing
International, 1997

Windows: Beautiful Curtains,
Shades, & Blinds You Can
Make
Meredith Books, 2001

Windows: How to Make
Curtains and Blinds
(Inspirations)
Alison Jenkins
Southwater, 2001

Windows: Recipes & Ideas:
Simple Solutions for the Home
Richard Lowther, et al
Chronicle Books, 2000

Windows with Style: Do-it-
yourself Window Treatments
Creative Publishing
International, 1997

Visual Index

11 12
13 14

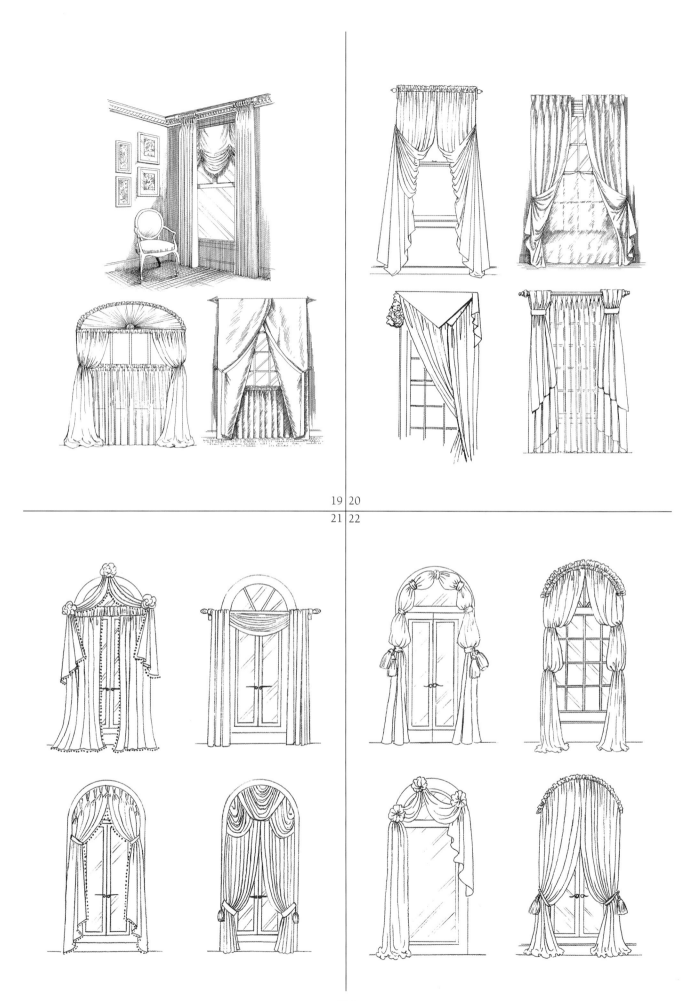

19	20
21	22

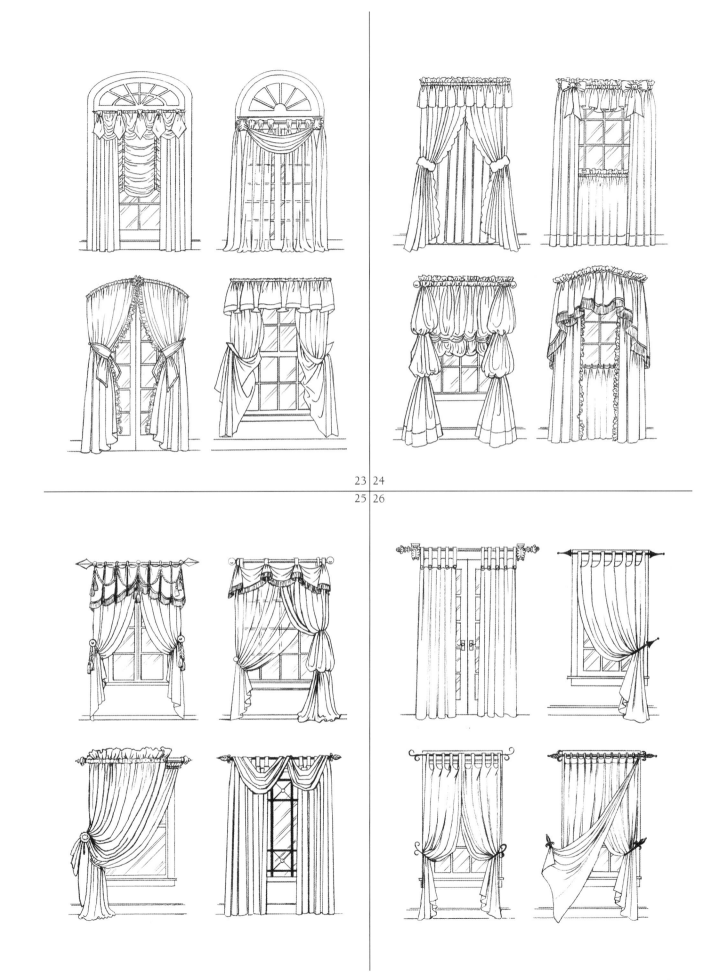

23 | 24
25 | 26

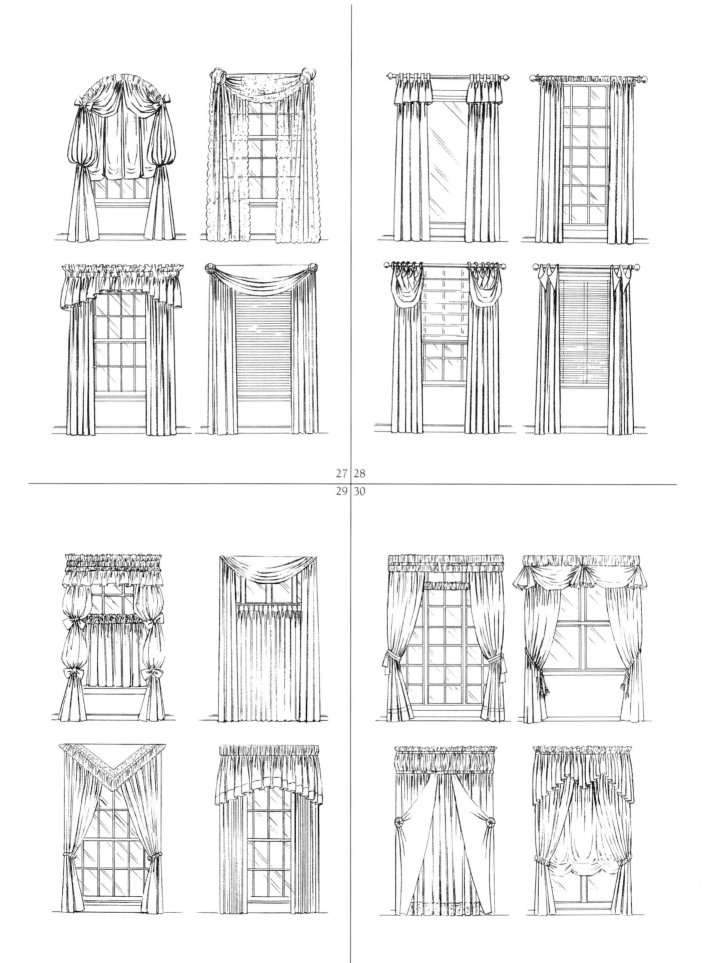

27 | 28
29 | 30

190

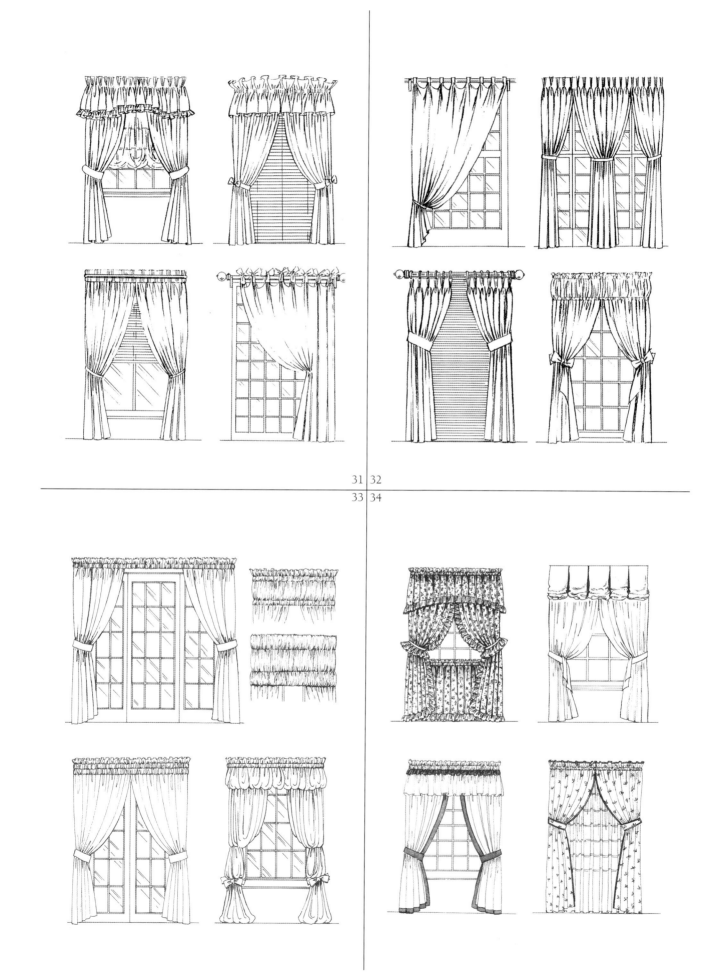

31 | 32
33 | 34

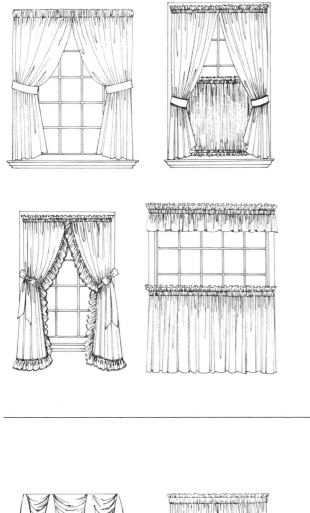

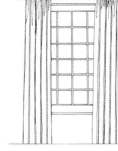

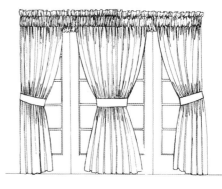

35 | 36
37 | 38

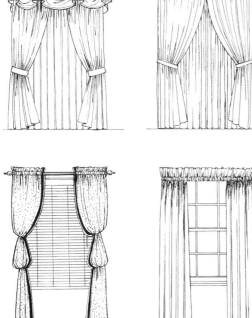

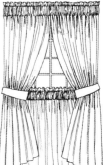

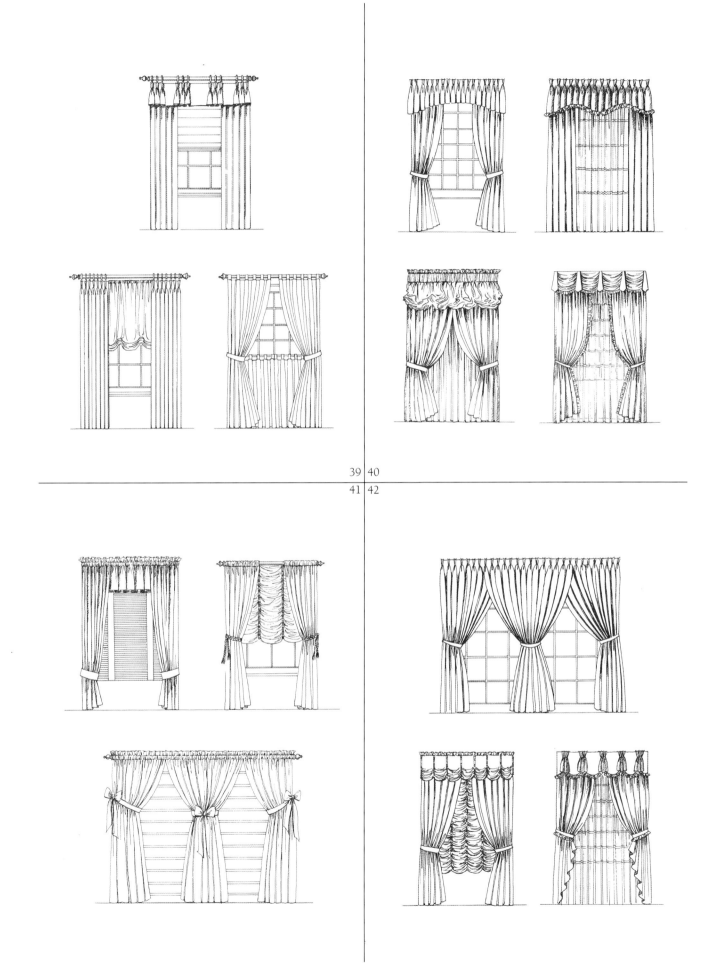

39 | 40

41 | 42

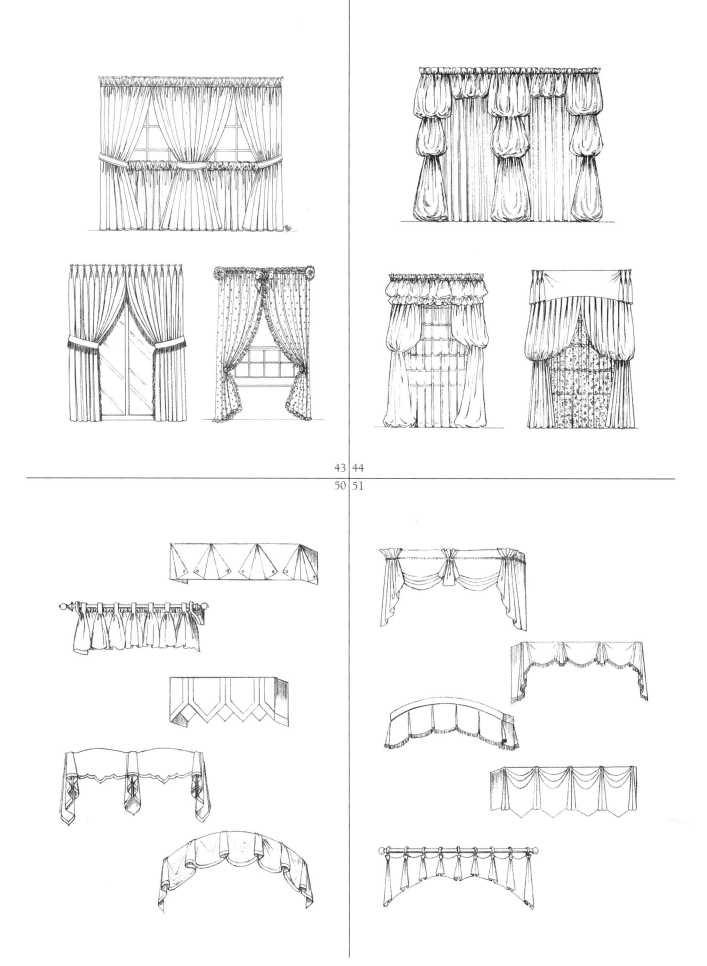

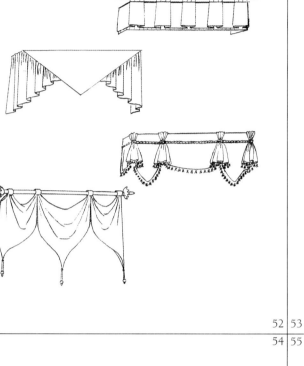

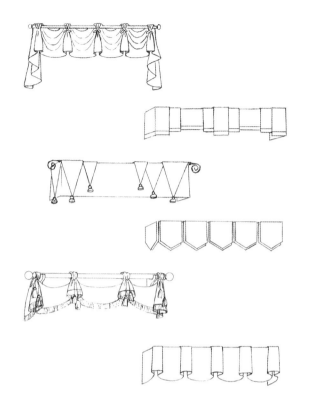

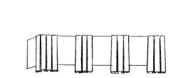

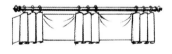

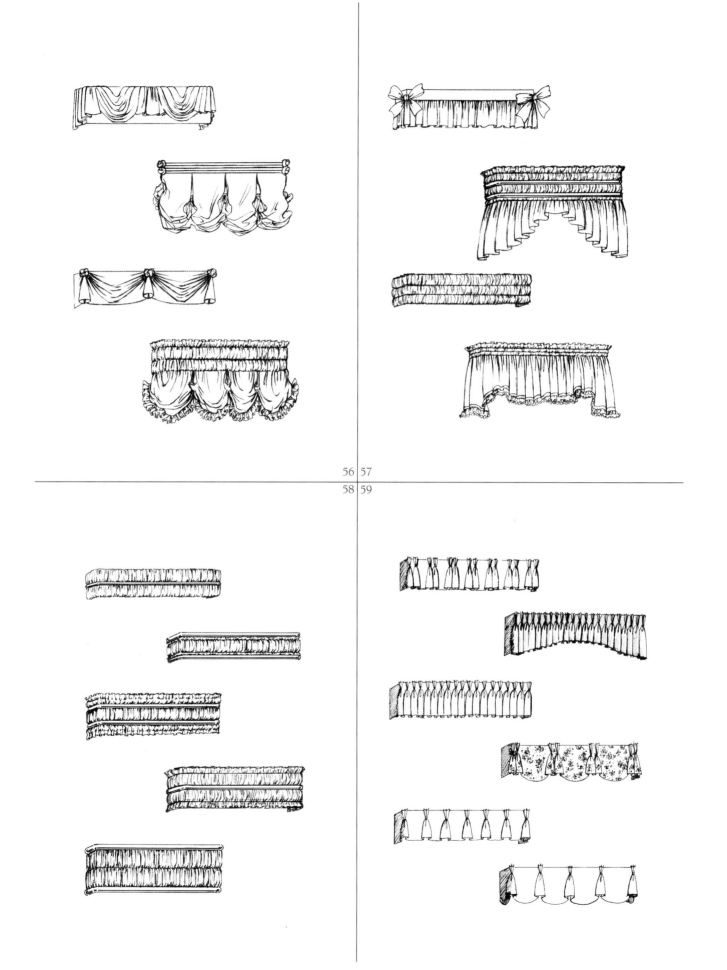

56 | 57
58 | 59

196

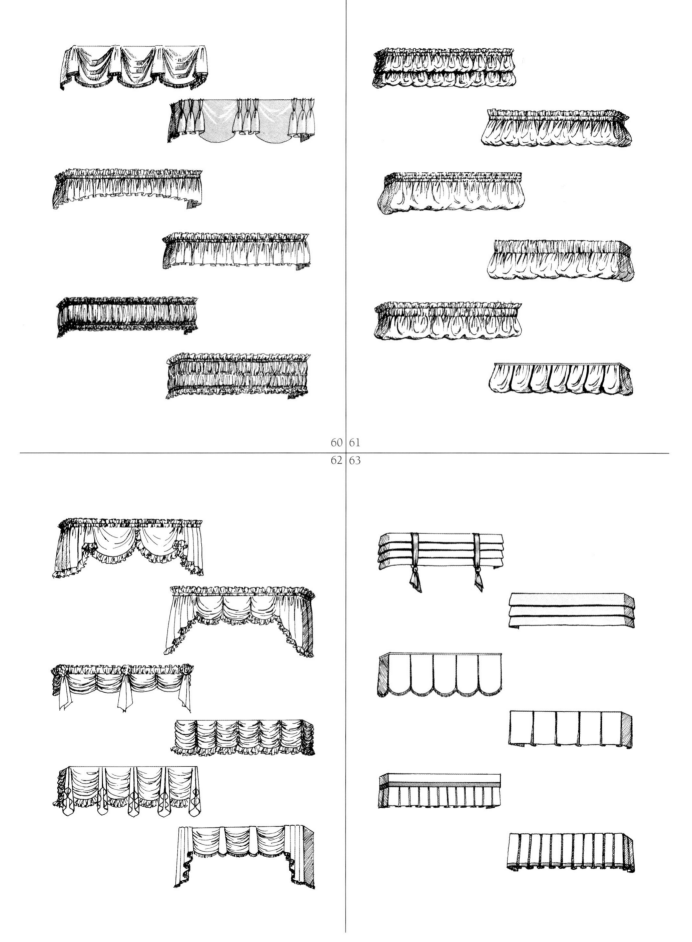

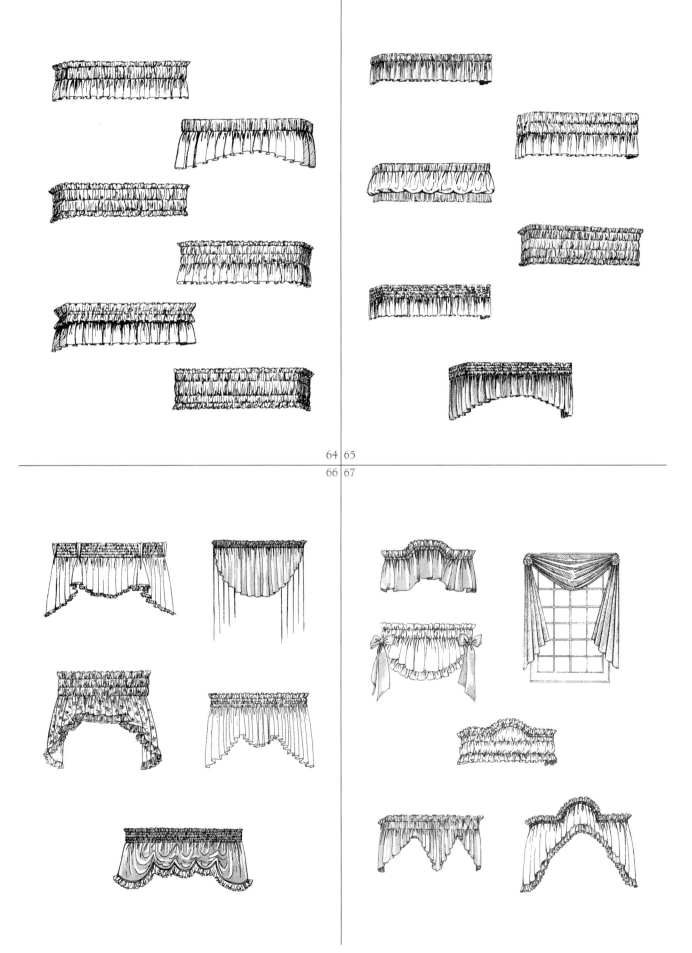

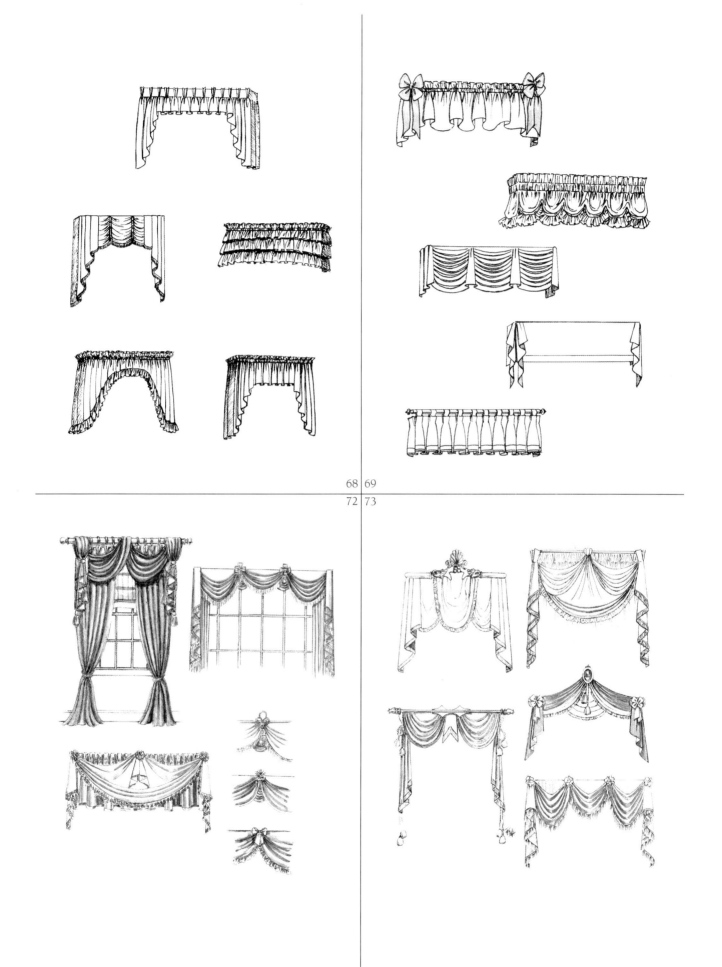

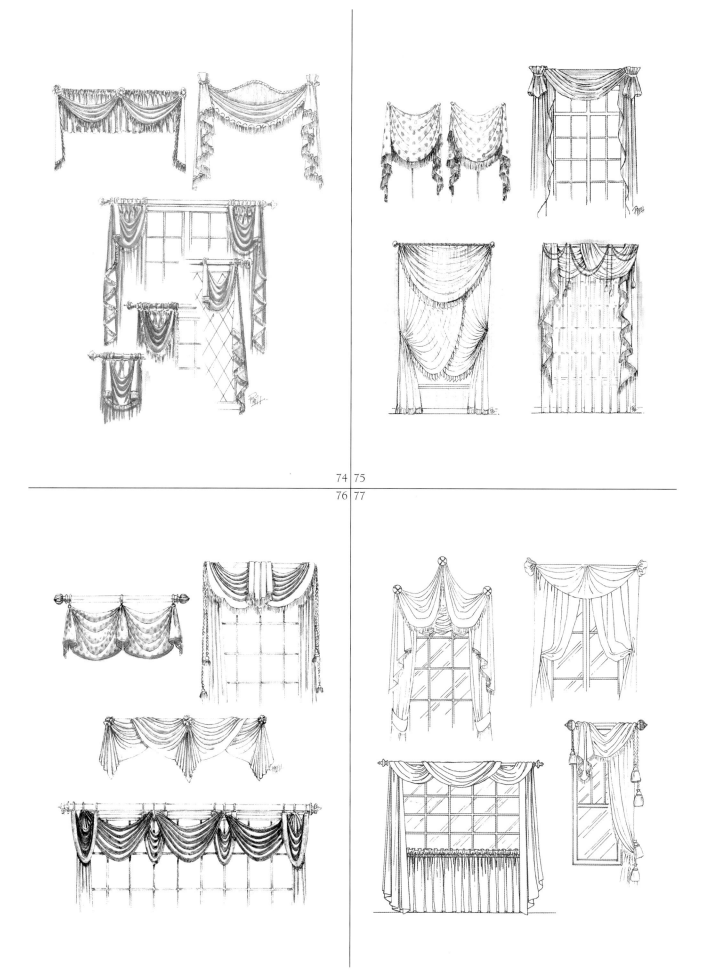

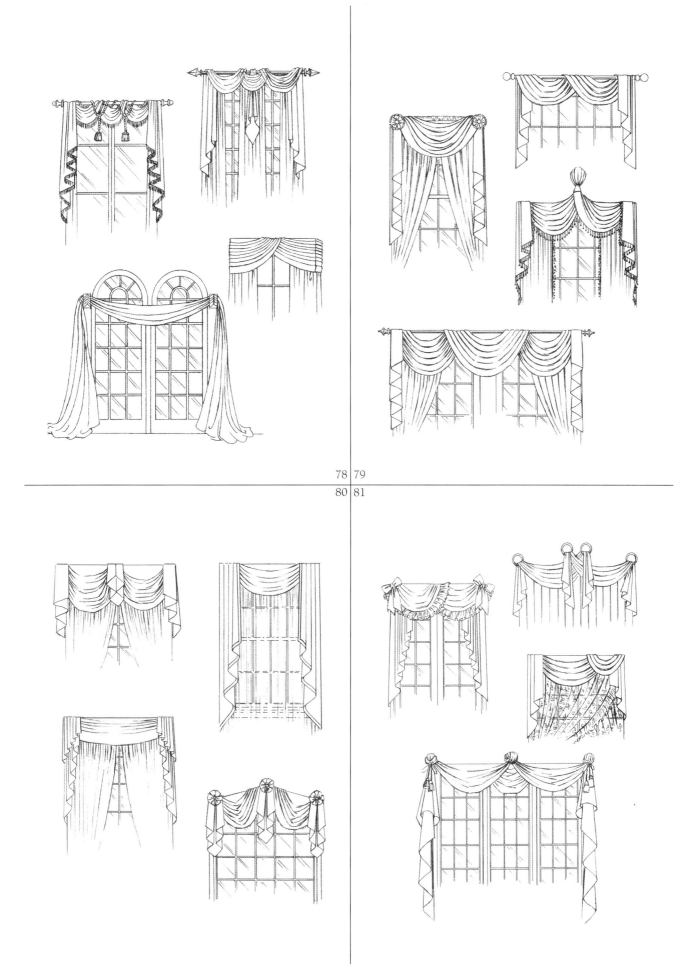

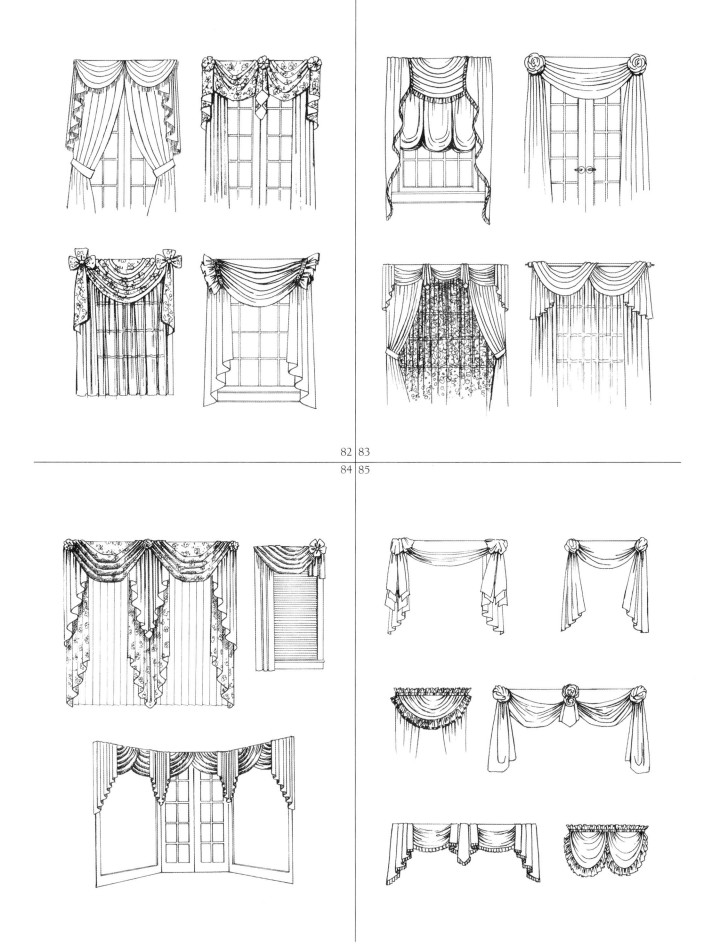

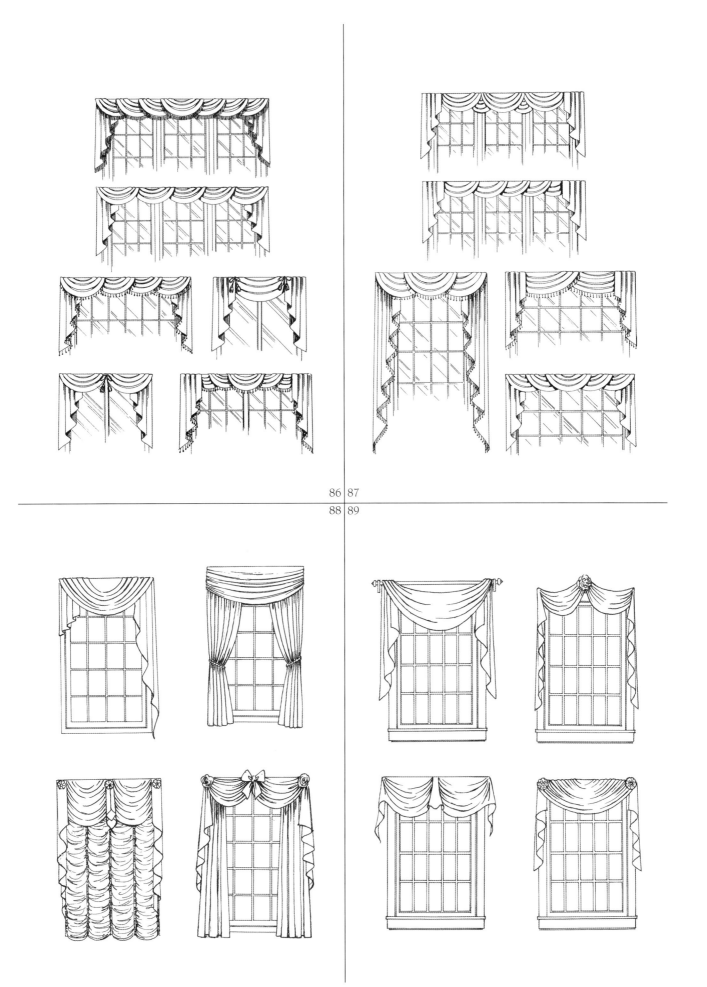

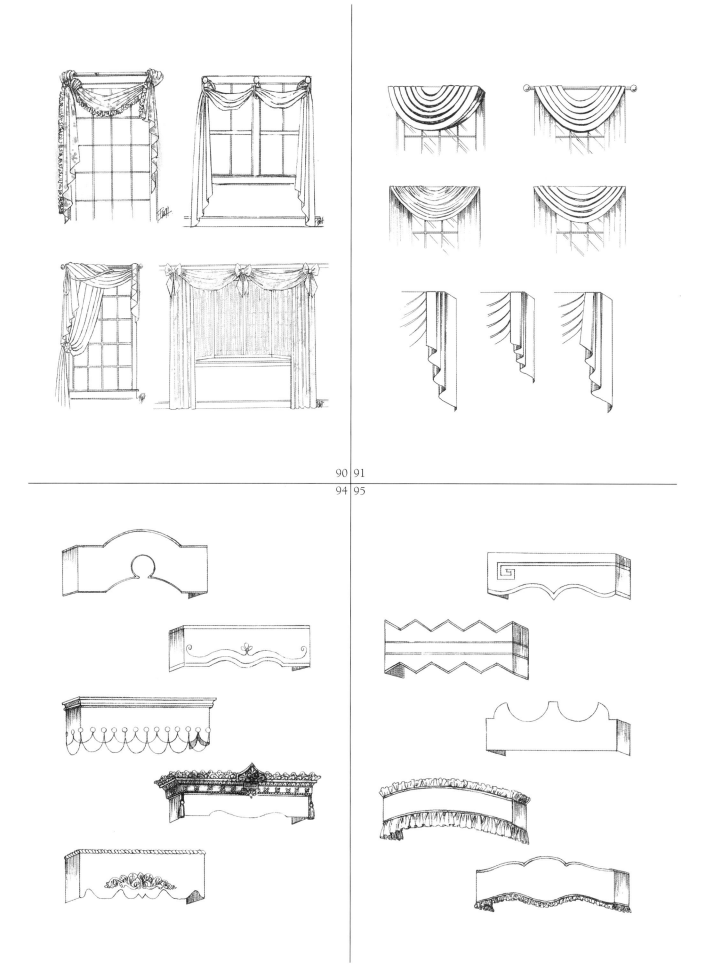

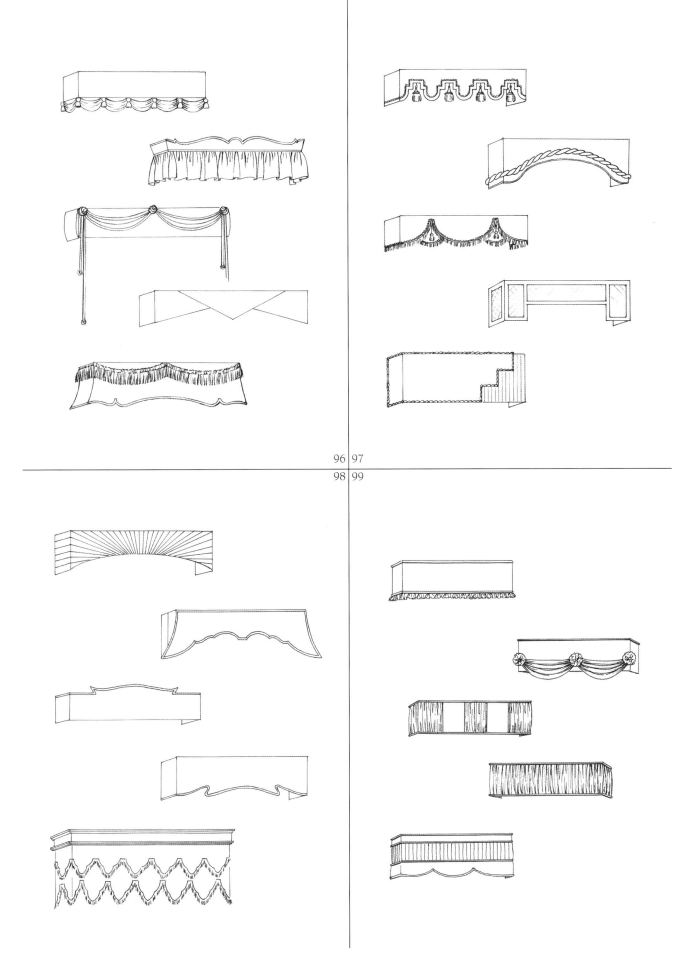

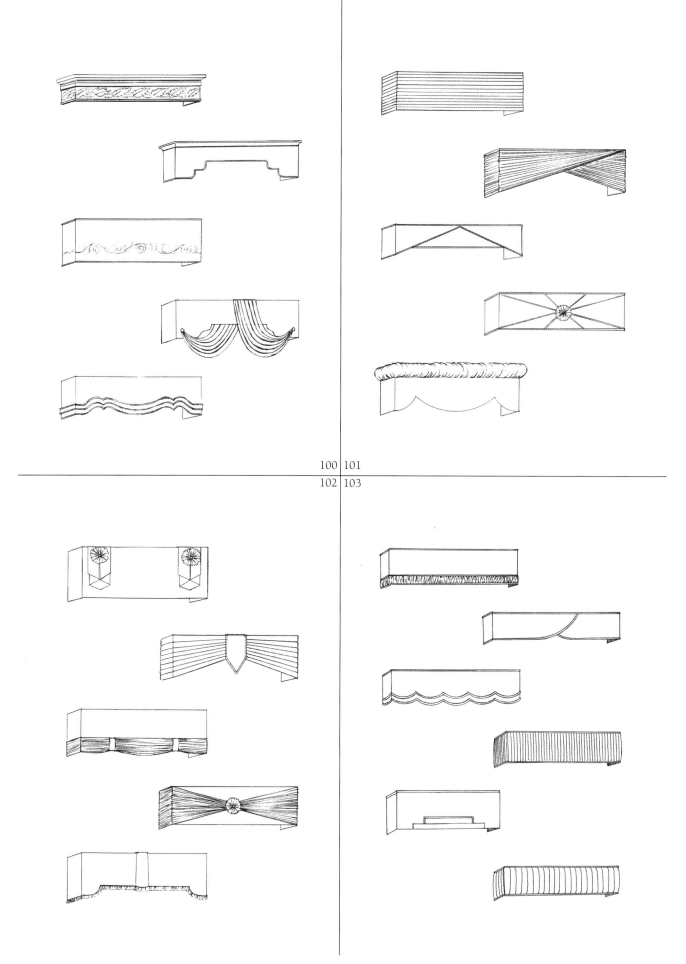

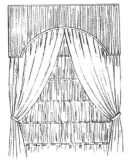

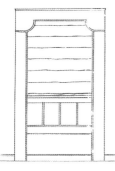

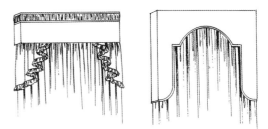

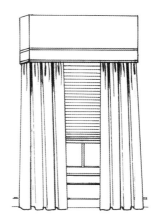

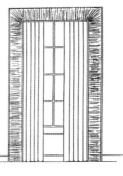

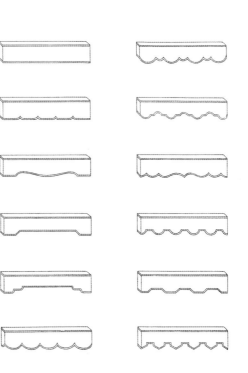

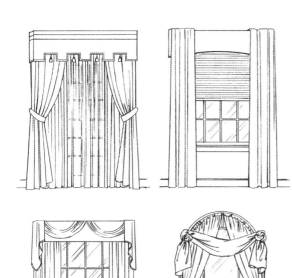

207

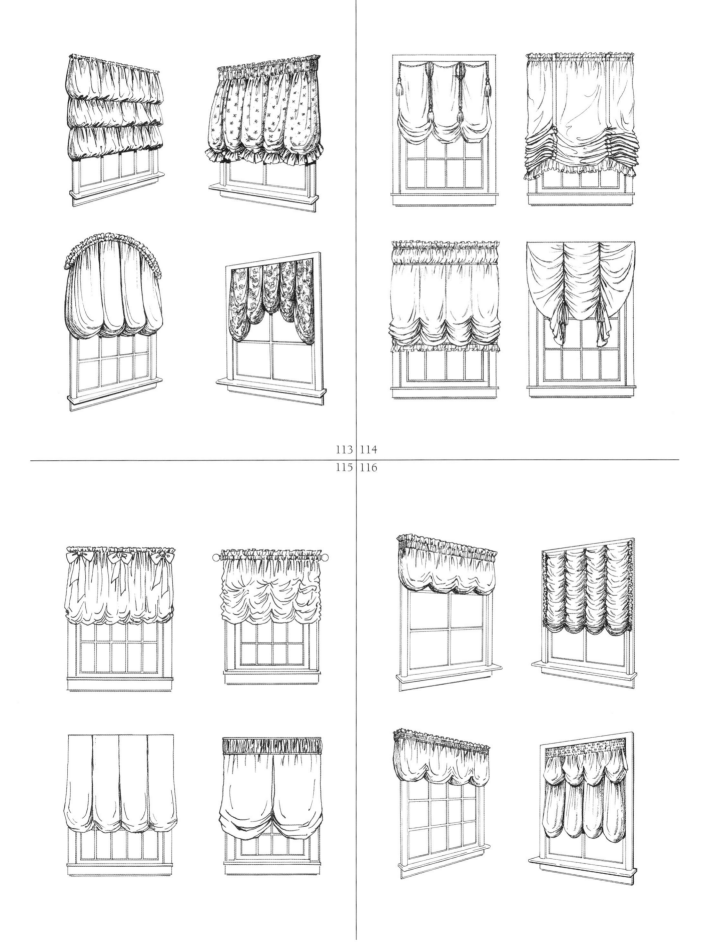

113 | 114
115 | 116

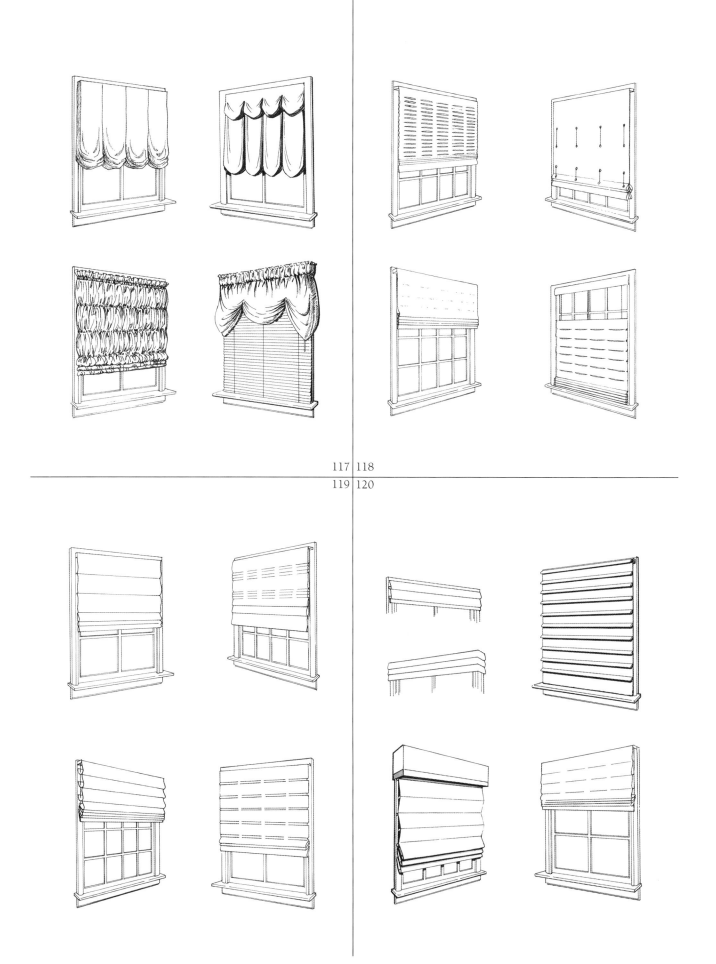

117 | 118
119 | 120

210

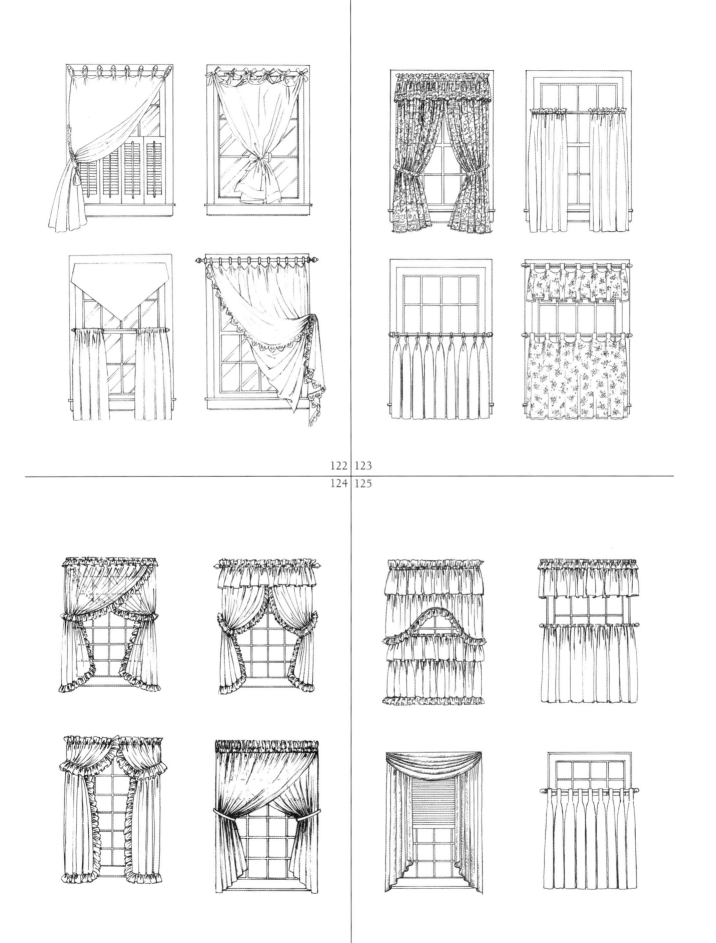

122 123
124 125

211

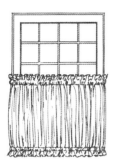

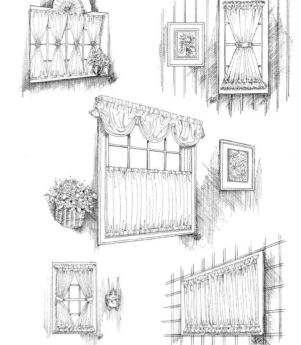

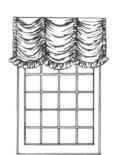

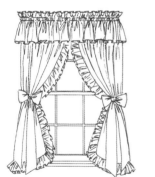

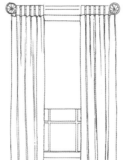

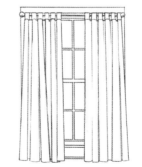

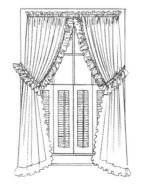

126 127
128 129

212

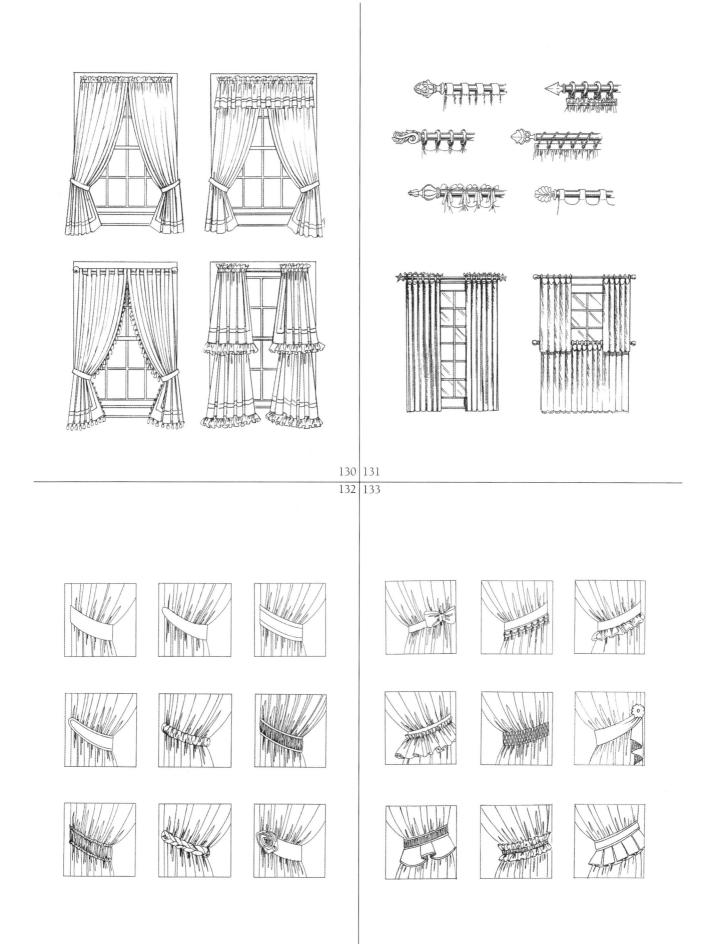

130 | 131
132 | 133

213

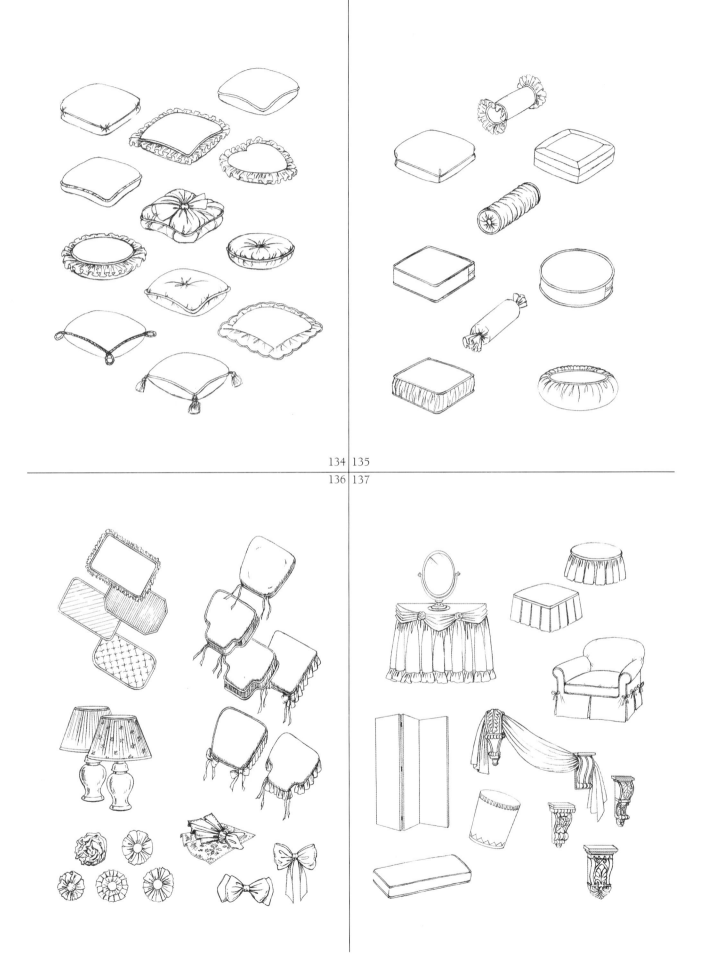

214

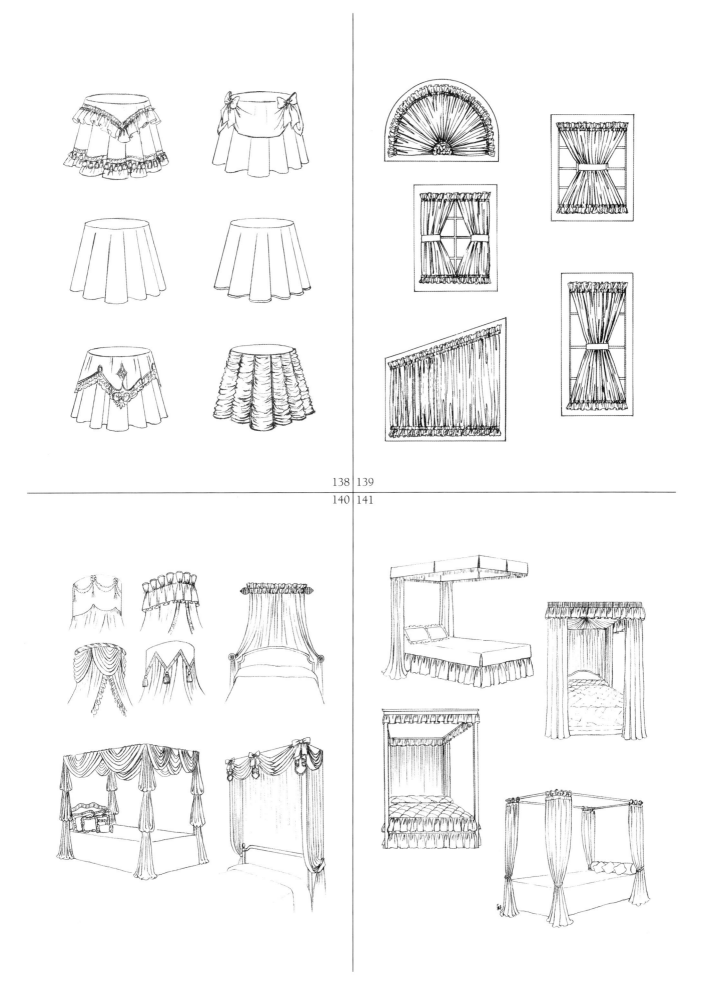

138 | 139
140 | 141

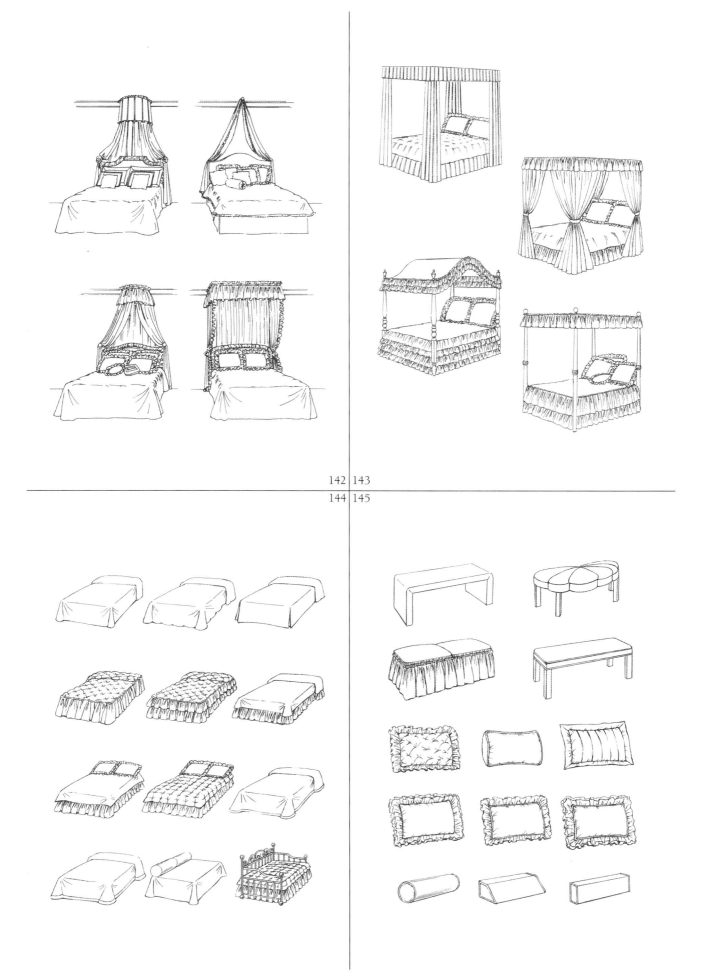

142 | 143

144 | 145

216

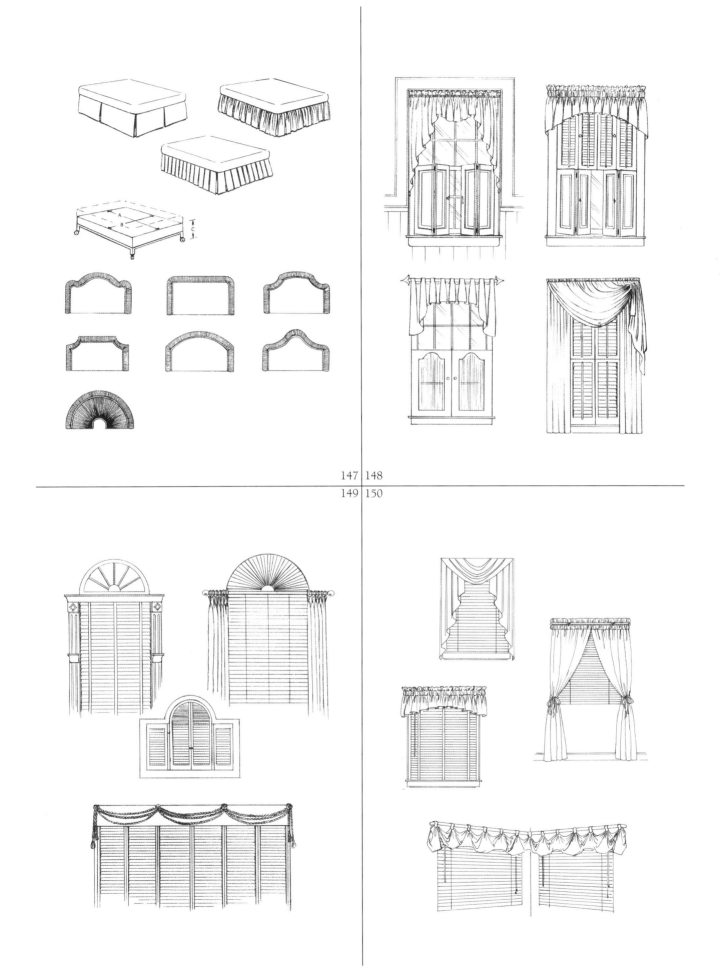

147 | 148
149 | 150

217

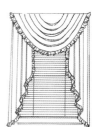

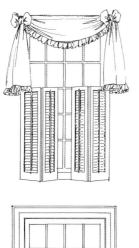
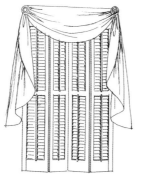

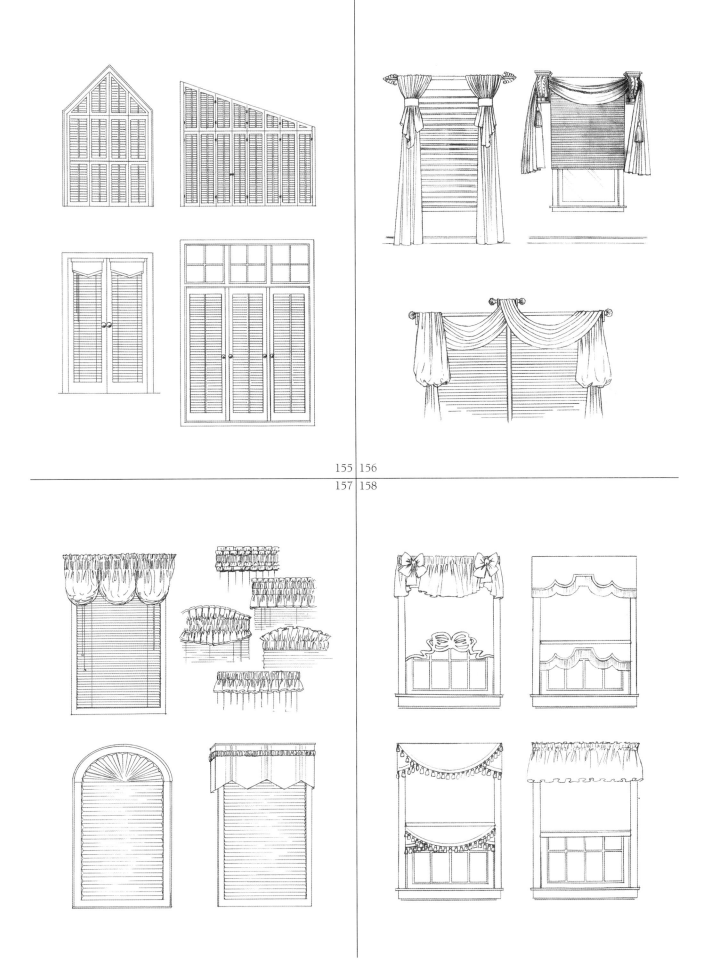

155 | 156
157 | 158

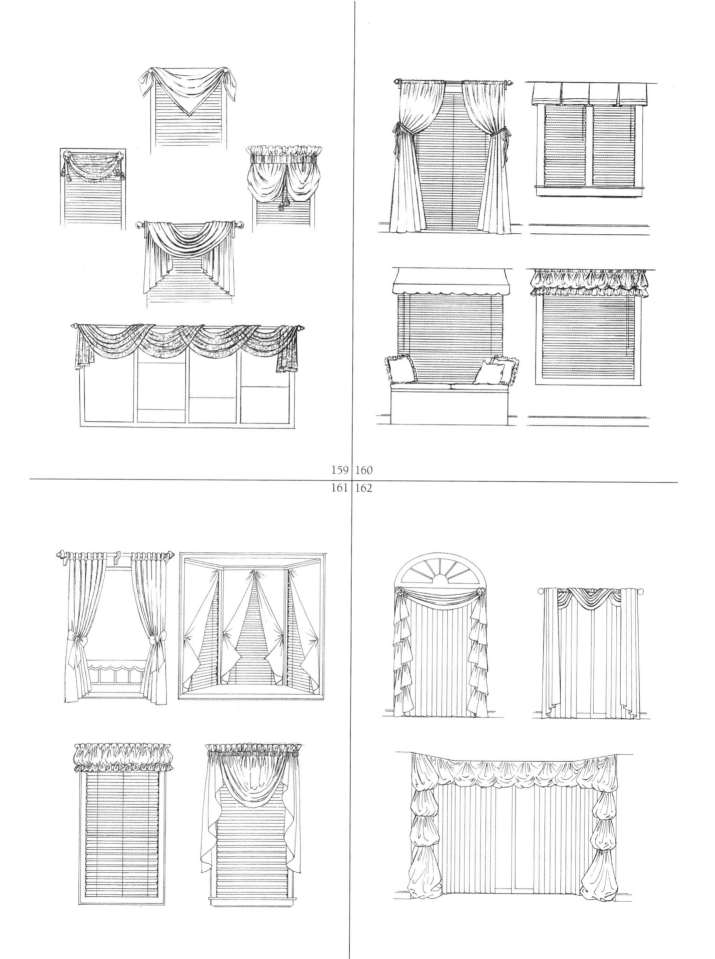

159 | 160

161 | 162

220

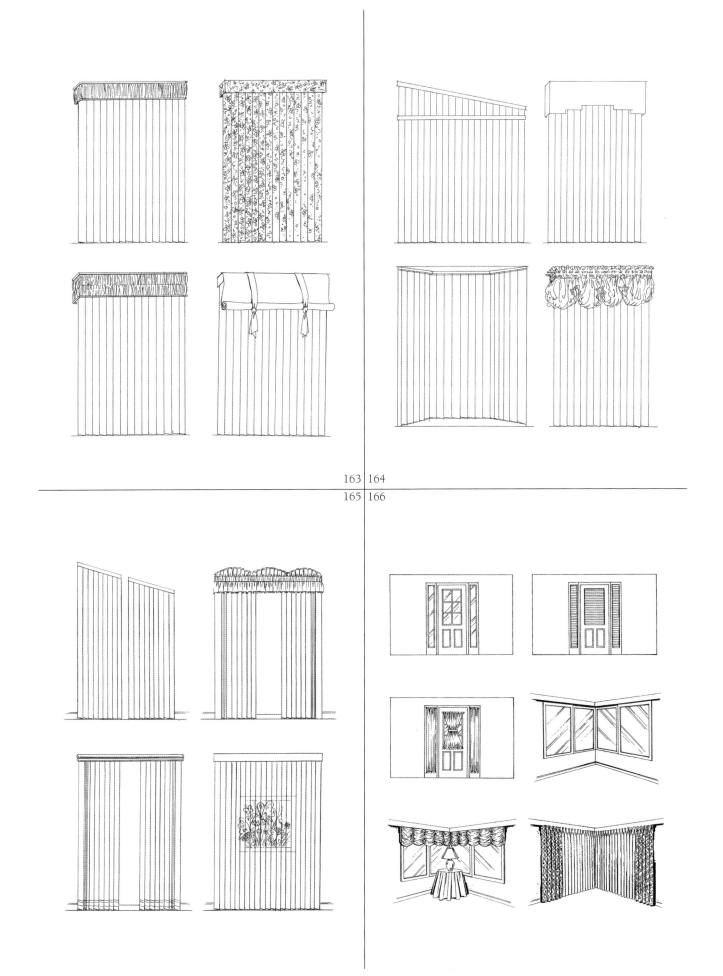

163 | 164
165 | 166

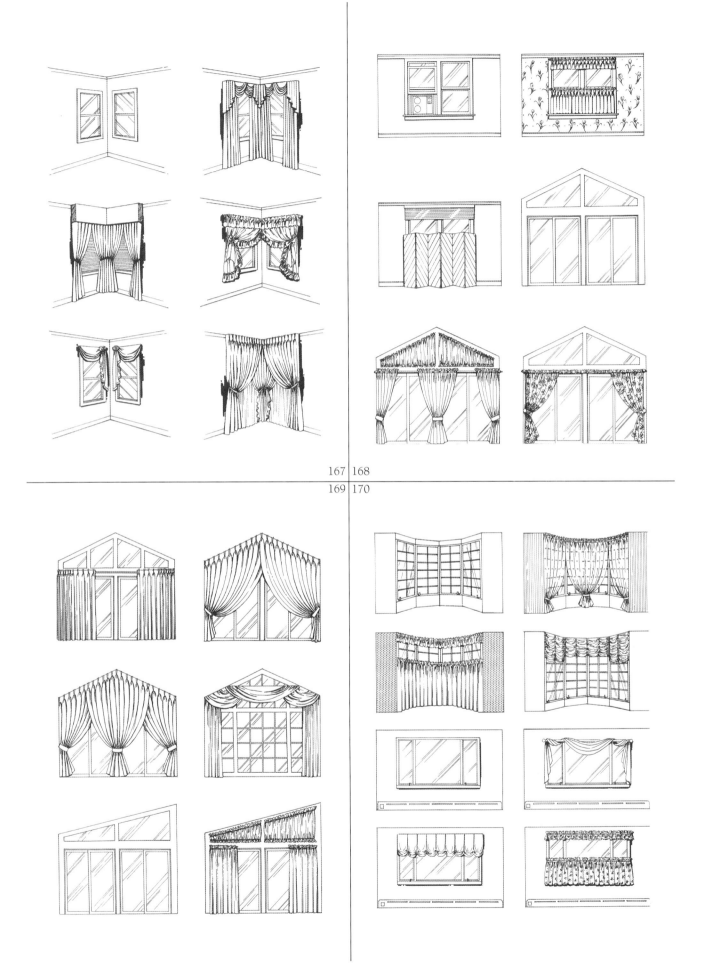

167 | 168
169 | 170

222

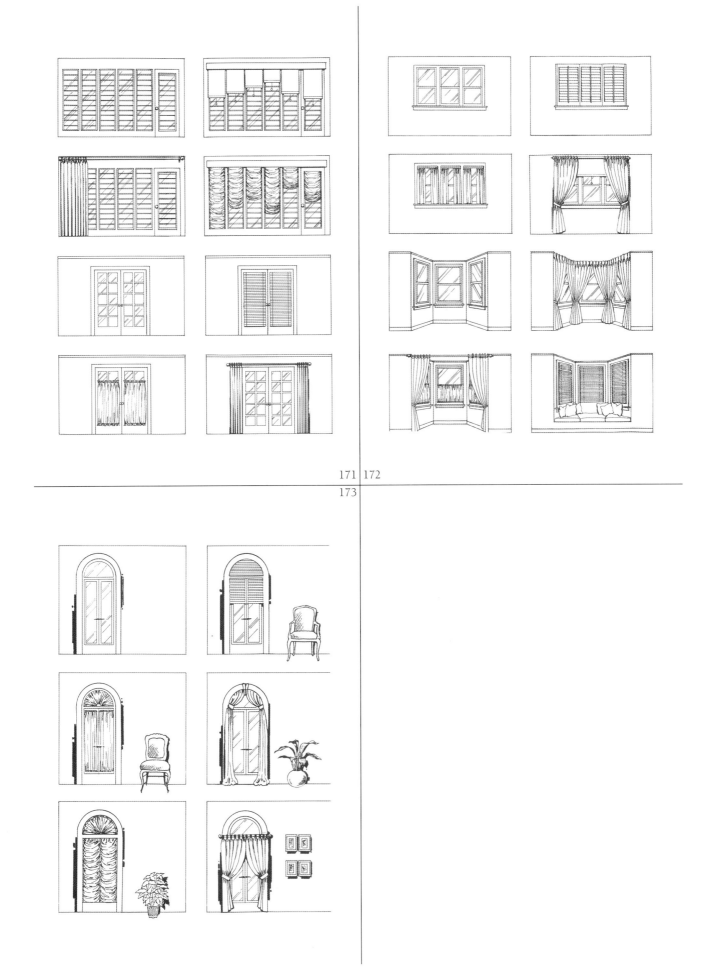

171 172
173

223

Index

Accessories 136, 137
Air Conditioner 168
American Early Georgian 9
American Federal 13
Angled
swag 80
top 101
Appliqué 94, 95
bottom 158
top 135
Arched 57, 125
canopy 143
cornice 94, 95, 97, 101, 102,
diagonally 101
double 30, 66, 67
draperies 19, 21-24, 27
heading 65
multiple 40, 54
rod pocket 64, 67, 129
shade 113, 157
shutters 149
sunburst 19
swags 21
valance 27, 30, 31, 34, 40,
50-52, 54, 57, 59, 60, 65, 66,
67, 69, 129, 150, 151
Arched Top 49, 113, 125,
157, 173
Arrangement Styles
swags and cascades 86, 87
Asymmetric
cascades 81, 84, 88
swags 13, 81, 90
tie back 20, 90
valance 17
Austrian Shade 23, 41, 42,
88, 116, 126
Austrian Valance 40, 42, 62,
68
Awning
valance 160
window 48
Balloon Drapery 44
Balloon Shade 27, 31, 39,
56, 83, 112-115, 128
swagged 117
wide pleated 112
Balloon Swag 85
Balloon Valance 34, 61, 152
Banding 23, 34, 50, 55, 63,
103, 105
bishops sleeve 37
cornice 94
edge 55
plain 69
raised 100
ribbon 130
shaped 100
tie backs 130
tie bands 132
valance 55, 69, 130
Baseboard Heater 170
Bay Window 48, 90, 162,
164, 170, 172
Bed Coverings 141
Bedspread 140, 141, 143
Benches
double 145

scalloped 145
upholstered 145
Bishop Sleeve 22, 37
draperies 24, 27, 29, 33, 38,
152
effect 162
valance 151
Blind 31, 119
mini 36, 37, 41, 117, 125,
157, 160
pleated 159
Venetian 150
vertical 162, 163, 164, 165
white wood 154
wood 149, 150, 151, 152,
155
Bolster 144
cylindrical 145
rectangular 145
wedge 145
Bottom-Up Shade 118
Bow Window 49
Bows 31, 38, 41, 43, 54, 57,
67, 69, 81, 88, 90, 115,
126, 128, 133, 136, 138,
158
Box Pleating 45, 63, 131
coverlet 141
tie 133
triple 55
valance 50-53, 55, 63, 142,
143, 152, 160
Boxed Swag Valance 88
Brass Rod 31, 125, 131, 165
Buttons 17, 50, 134
Café Curtain 19, 20, 24, 29,
34, 36, 39, 43, 122, 123,
125, 126
double 131
Canopy 143
Cantonniere 110
Cascades 56, 62, 68, 72, 73,
78-81, 83, 85- 87, 92, 105,
106, 133, 140, 161
arrangement styles 86, 87
asymmetric 81, 84, 88
double 79
empire 75
formal 82
inverted 77
long 84
stacked 91
standard 91
tails 89
yardage requirements 93
Cascading Effect 119
Casement Windows 48, 170
Cathedral Top 67
Cathedral Windows 49, 155,
168, 169
Ceiling Mounted Valance
141
Center Florence 41
Center Sleeve 33
Clerestory Windows 49, 155,
169
Cloud Shade 19, 30, 112-116,
159

Cloud Valance 40, 56, 61, 65,
66, 127, 151, 154, 157
Cluster 39
Comforter
tufted 144
Contrasting Lining 89
Cord 75, 118
double knotted 56
knotted 56
shirred 132
trim 90
twisted 55
welt 132
Corner Gliding Windows 166
Corner Windows 49, 168
Cornice Box Shapes 107-
109
Cornice Boxes 94, 95, 99-
103, 105-109, 111, 149, 154
angled top 101
button swagged 96
chevron 95, 96
crown 96, 98
custom 95, 98
designer 74, 94
measuring information 111
multi-fabric 97
narrow 57
pagoda 95, 96, 98
scalloped 101, 103
shaped 96, 97, 98, 105
shirred 99, 103, 104, 115,
163
soft 53, 54, 106
straight 96, 98, 100, 101, 102
sunburst 98
wood 94, 100
Country 43
Covered Rod 37, 79
Coverlet 142, 143
box pleated 141
plain 144
quilted 143, 144
Crown 140
cameo 73
custom 149
shaped 98
shell 73
wood 98
Curtains 49, 122
banded 130
lace 44
Priscilla 124
rod top 124
straight 129
tab tied 131
tabbed 122, 161
tab-top 128, 129, 130
threaded 129
tie backs 123, 124, 126, 128,
129, 130, 161
tiered 130
café 19, 20, 24, 29, 34, 35,
39, 43, 122, 123, 125, 126,
128, 131
Custom
cornice 95
draperies 45

shutters 155
Day Bed 144
Decorator Pole 38, 41, 142
Decorator Rod 16, 19, 25,
26, 28, 32, 38, 39, 50, 53,
55, 57, 58, 69, 76-79, 122,
124, 126, 128, 129, 140,
150, 156, 159, 160
brass 125, 131
gold 73
Designer
cloud shade 112
cornice 74, 94
touch 163
Diamond Rod Pocket
127, 139
Divider 137
Dormer Window 48
Double Cascades 79, 92
Double Hung Window 48,
168, 172
triple 172
Double Rod Pocket 25, 33,
44, 60, 64, 65, 66, 114
Double Swags 79, 80, 81, 83,
84, 85, 89, 150
Double Window 49
Draped
crossed in middle 81
over holdbacks 142
over rod 79, 83
swag 83, 89, 150
through sconces 78
valance 89
Draperies 19, 20, 27-30, 38,
40, 41, 76, 90, 105, 126,
148, 149, 156
balloon 44
custom made 45
double rod pocket 33
flat rod pocket 35, 36
how to order 45
lace 27
measurements 45
options available 45
stationary 37, 38, 143
terminology 45
rod pocket 18, 21-25, 32-37,
44, 127
tent 19, 20
tie backs 19, 20, 25, 29-35,
37, 38, 40-44
pleated 16, 17, 20, 21, 25,
32, 39, 42, 43, 72, 73
bishop sleeve 22, 24, 27, 29,
33, 37, 38, 152
tab 16, 23, 25, 26, 28, 31,
32, 39
Dust Ruffle
box pleated 143, 147
shirred 144, 147
tailored 142, 147
Early Georgian 8
Edge
banding 55
fringed 63
knife 134
pleated 85

pouffed 117
ruffled 115
scalloped 42, 144
welt 134, 138
Empire Valance 69
End-Pleated Valance 44
English Baroque 8
English Middle Georgian 9
English Neoclassic 12
European 75
Fabric
covered 137
draped 137, 142, 150, 156
draped through sconces 78, 137
folded over decorator rod 156
insert 103, 111, 148, 153, 163
multi-fabric 65, 97
pleated 99
shades 114
swagged 75, 90, 152, 159, 162
ties 90
triple fullness 116, 117
Flat Rod 56-58
Flat Rod Pocket 35, 36
Florence 41
Folds 20, 119, 120
French 7
French Doors 49, 84, 155, 171
shutters 154
French Neoclassic 11
French Pleated 123
draperies 39
valance 17, 40, 59, 68
Fringe 43, 51, 62, 63, 78, 96, 97, 98, 133, 158, 159
Full Tie Back 75
Fullness Chart 46
Gathered 69, 101, 115-117
canopy 143
cascade 91, 161
cornice 101, 111, 163
curtain 122
double 31, 163
draperies 20, 21, 23, 38, 41, 126, 151
dust ruffle 143
heading 131
panels 106
swag 73, 91, 161
triple 57
valance 27, 29, 30, 31, 52, 54, 57, 58, 96, 123, 125, 143, 150, 153, 158, 160
Glass Wall 49
Grommets 131
brass 118
Headboard
upholstered 140, 142, 147
Heading 33, 45, 51, 60, 122, 131
box pleated 131
buckram 45
double 45
gathered with rings 131
gilded 73
gold leaf 106

grommet 131
rod pocket 61, 65
rope 131
scalloped 131
shirred 61, 65, 66
tab 131
ties 131
Heart Shaped 134
High Rod 123
Historical Window Treatments 6
American Early Georgian 9
American Federal 13
Early Georgian 8, 9
English Baroque 8
English Middle Georgian 9
English Neoclassic 12
French Neoclassic 11
Italian French Renaissance 7
Louis XV 10
Louis XVI 11
Neoclassic 11-13
Rococo 10
Victorian 14, 15
Holdbacks 26, 122, 142
Horizontal Rods 117
Hourglass 102, 127, 139
Inside Installation 121
In-Swinging Casement 48
Inverted Cascade 77
Inverted Pleats 117
box 63
Italian 7
Jabots 54, 62, 69, 75, 82, 83, 92, 102, 140, 151
effect 75
Jalousie Window 48, 171
Kingston Valance 37, 50, 53, 60
Knots 21, 22, 27, 54, 56, 81, 96, 106, 134
Knotted Scarf Swag 21
Knotted Swag 21, 22, 27, 106
Lace
curtain 44, 129
draperies 27
multiple 159
panels 83
table cover 138
tie backs 150, 160
valance 129
Lambrequin 56, 104, 110
Lamp Shades 136
Leaded Glass 154
Leaf Design
gold 106
painted 100
Louis XV 10
valance 50
Louis XVI 11
Maltese Cross Ties 72, 82, 140
Measuring Information
cornice boxes 111
draperies 45
dust ruffles 147
headboards 147
shades 121
Mini Blind 36, 37, 41, 117, 125, 157, 160

Mini-Pleats 118, 119
Molding
custom 149
Murphy Valance 51
Napkin Rings 136
Napkins 136
Natural Finish
wood blind 154
Neck Roll 135
Neoclassic 13
English 12
French 11
Ottoman
round 137
square 137
Outside Installation 121
Out-Swinging Casement 48
Overlay 138
Palladian Window 49
Panels 36, 45, 83, 99, 106, 116, 119, 141
Picture Window 48
Picture Window 48, 170
Pillows
sham 145
throw 134, 135
Pinch Pleated 43, 45
double 59
Piping 61
Placemats 136
Pleat Spacing 45
Pleat To Chart 46
Pleating 51, 99, 102, 103, 111, 133
alternate 119
blind 159
box 45, 51, 52, 53, 55, 63, 131, 142, 152
cluster 39
cornice 102, 111
curtains 125
diagonally arched 101
double 59
draperies 16, 17, 20, 21, 25, 32, 39, 42, 43, 45, 72, 73, 104
edge 85
end 44
French 17, 39, 40, 59, 68, 123
goblet 16
honeycomb 101
horizontal 119
inverted 117
mini 119
pinch 43, 45, 59
shade 112, 117, 119, 156-158, 160, 161
space 42, 59, 60, 66
spacing 45
swag 91
tie back 42, 133
valance 16, 17, 31, 39, 40, 42, 44, 50, 51, 52, 53, 55, 59, 60, 68, 72, 142, 152, 165
Pole 115, 116
Pouffed 117
Priscilla Curtains 124
Puffed
tie Backs 44
valance 161

Pull Down 43
Pulled Back
draperies 30
panels 161
Queen Ann Valance 42, 52, 59, 60
Quilted
bedspread 141
coverlet 143
sham 145
throw 144
Ranch Window 48
Renaissance
French Italian 7
Repeating Pattern 119
Return 45
Ribbon 130
Rings 81, 90, 123, 131
Rococo 10
Rod Pocket 45, 64, 124
café 35, 36
diamond 127, 139
double 25, 33, 44, 60, 61, 64, 65, 66, 114
flat 35, 36
hourglass 127, 139
shade 114, 117
slant top 127, 139
sunburst 139
swag 62
tie backs 35
top 124
triple 65
Rod Pocket Drapery 17, 21-25, 32-37, 44, 127, 140
double 25, 33
flat 35, 36
Rod Pocket Valance 35, 36, 40, 60, 61, 62, 64, 66, 67, 68, 74, 141, 142, 148, 158
arched 54, 60, 64, 65, 129
ceiling mounted 141
double 44, 60, 61, 64, 65
triple 65
Roller Shades 158, 161
Roman Shade 17, 39, 41, 72, 104, 118-120
mini fold 120
mock 63
Roman Valance 120
mock 63
Rope 25, 52, 77, 78, 94, 96, 114, 131, 149
twisted 97
Rosettes 27, 43, 73, 79, 80, 82, 84, 85, 88, 99, 101, 102, 132, 136, 142
Ruffles 23, 34, 35, 56, 57, 66, 68, 81, 83, 99, 124, 126, 151
arched 57
bedspread 143
bottom 113, 144
cascade 105
cornice 95
double 64, 133, 141
edge 115
pillow 134, 135, 145
side drops 162
skirt 138
standup 61, 64, 69

sunburst 19
swag 85, 153
tie 133
tie backs 34, 43, 128, 129, 142
top 116, 159
valance 64, 142, 161
Sashes 48
Scalloped
bench 145
bottom 101, 103
edge 42, 144
heading 131
panels 116
ruffle 134
shade 158
top 131, 144
valance 53, 63, 123, 160, 165
Sconces 26, 78, 137
Seat Cushions 136, 137
Shades 156, 157, 160, 161
Austrian 41, 42, 88, 116, 126
balloon 27, 31, 39, 56, 112-115, 117, 128
bottom-up 118
cloud 19, 30, 112-116, 159
dramatic accordion look 118
measuring information 121
nautical 118
pull down 43
roller 158, 161
Roman 17, 39, 41, 72, 118-120
specialty soft 114
stagecoach 112
Sheers 20, 24, 25, 29, 31, 34, 37, 40, 42, 44, 77, 123
Shirred 64, 99
Austrian 138
band 103, 105
cord 132
cornice 99, 104, 115, 163
curtain 123, 126
drop 144
dust ruffle 144
fabric insert 153
heading 61, 65
lambrequin 104
pillow 134, 135
rod 162
shade 116
skirt 145
tie bands 132, 133
valance 66, 151, 164
Shutters 122, 129, 149, 153
arched 149
café 153
custom fitted 155
fabric insert 148
French door 154, 155
full 153
half 151
louvered 148, 153
plantation 151
solid wood 148
sunburst 154
traditional 148, 155

wide blade 154
Side Drops 97, 105, 152, 162
Sidelights 166
Single Cascade 81, 92
Single Swag 27, 29, 79, 80, 89
Slant
rod pocket 127
verticals 164
window 49, 155, 165
Sleeve 28, 33, 38
Sliding Glass Doors 49, 168
Slip Covered Chair 137
Smocked 116
Space Pleated 42, 59, 60, 66
Special Swag Effect 28, 75
Specialty Soft Shade 114
Stack Back Chart 46
Stagecoach Shade 112
Stagecoach Valance 54, 163
Stand-up 36, 37, 61, 64, 69
Stationary 37, 38, 143
Stationary Drapery 37, 38, 143
Strip Window 48
Structural Beam 166
Studio Couch 144
Sunburst 19, 139
shutter 154
Suspender Balloon Shade 114
Swagged Valance 30
box 88
double 89
Swags 16, 21, 23, 29, 54, 56, 72-74, 77, 78-89, 99, 140, 151, 152, 159, 162
arched 21
arrangement styles 86, 87
asymmetrical 13, 81, 90
deep 75
draped 83, 89
empire 75, 76, 92
fan 73
formal 82
gathered 73, 82, 91, 161
in and out 100
joined in middle 79
knotted 21, 22, 27, 106
knotted scarf 21
open 76, 91
raised 77
short 159
special 75
traditional 67, 125
turban 78
two-tone 153
waterfall 76
wrapped 91
yardage requirements 92, 93
Tab Draperies 16, 23, 25, 26, 28, 31, 32
double 26
Tab Valance 17, 25, 50, 52, 53, 69, 150
Tabbed Curtain 122, 125, 128, 129, 130, 131, 161
Table Covers 138
Tassel 16, 25, 73, 75, 77, 81,

97, 114, 134, 138, 149, 159
Tear Drop Valance 16, 52
Throw Pillows 134, 135
Throw Spread 142, 144
Tie Backs 19, 20, 29-35, 40-42, 44, 77, 85, 90, 104, 128-130, 142, 143
curtains 123, 124, 126, 130, 161
full 75
lace 150, 160
multiple 43
draperies 17, 25, 32, 34, 35, 40, 42
Tie-Bands 36, 38, 54, 132, 133
Tiers 80, 113, 130
Ties 23, 41, 54, 63, 85, 90, 106, 112, 124, 131 133, 138
Time Line 6
Trim 53
brass 165
cord 90
tassel 75
welt 145
Triple Draped Swags 79
Triple Fullness Fabric 116, 117
Turban 78
Upholstered
headboards 140, 142, 147
Valance 27-31, 33-36, 50-52, 54, 55, 57-64, 66-71, 88, 89, 96, 120, 123-125, 129, 130, 142, 148, 158, 161
Austrian 40, 42, 62, 68
Awning 160
balloon 34, 61, 152
banner 53
bishops sleeve 151
Bordeaux 51
canopy 143
cathedral top 67
ceiling mounted 141
chevron 122, 155
cloud 40, 56, 61, 65, 66, 69, 127, 151, 154, 157, 164
empire 69
full 160
geometric 157
half-round 142
handkerchief 20, 52
Kingston 37, 50, 53, 60
lambrequin 56
Louis XV 50
matching 116, 117
multi-level 53
multiple point 51, 55
Murphy 51
New Orleans 68
open 53
overlapping 120
petticoat 68
pointed 16, 50
Queen Ann 42, 52, 59, 60
regal 53
rolled 54
Roman 63, 120
shaped 56

spacer 66
stagecoach 54, 163
tapered 55, 62, 66, 67, 68
tear drop 16, 52
triple cone 55
Vanity Table 137
Venetian Blind 150
Ventilation 48
Verticals 162, 163-165
Victorian 14, 15
Wastebasket 137
Welting 101, 132, 133, 135, 144
edge 134, 138
pillow sham 145
rope 134
special 103
trim 145
Window Types 48
Wood
blinds 149, 151, 152, 154, 155
header 100
shutters 148
Venetian blind 150
Yardage Information 46
bed coverings 146
cascades 92, 93
headings chart 47
swags 93